Brachiosaurus

Spinosaurus

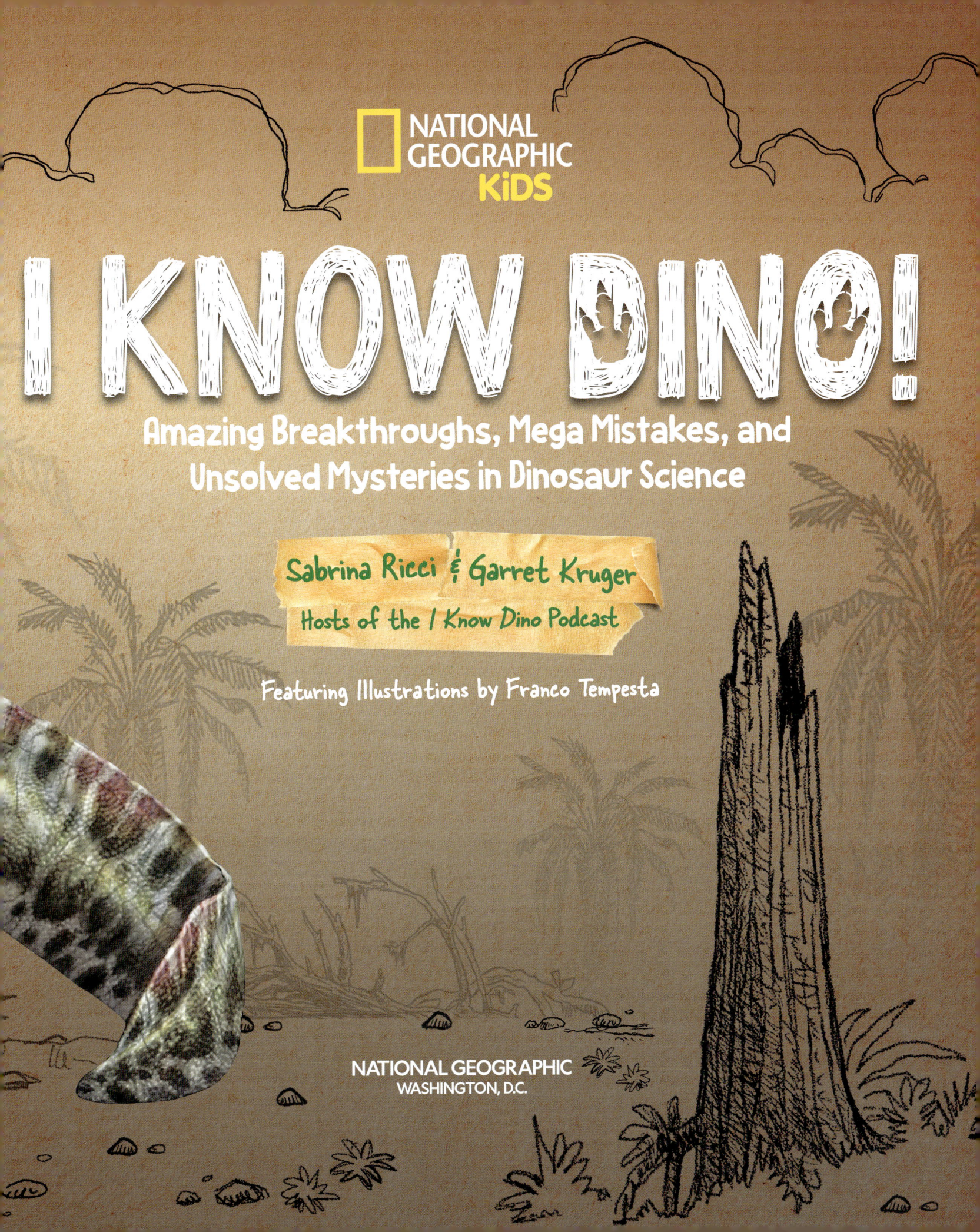

NATIONAL GEOGRAPHIC
KiDS

I KNOW DINO!

Amazing Breakthroughs, Mega Mistakes, and Unsolved Mysteries in Dinosaur Science

Sabrina Ricci & Garret Kruger

Hosts of the *I Know Dino* Podcast

Featuring Illustrations by Franco Tempesta

NATIONAL GEOGRAPHIC
WASHINGTON, D.C.

CONTENTS

Sinosauropteryx

INTRODUCTION

If dinosaurs were featured in a wildlife yearbook, they'd get all the awards: largest animal to walk on Earth, biggest claws, longest neck, and many others.

Dinosaurs were so dominant that our mammal ancestors basically hid in burrows for the whole Mesozoic Era (see chart), mostly sneaking out at night. Dinosaurs were so impressive that we are still talking about them over 66 million years after they disappeared! Although technically dinosaurs are still around today—as birds.

Dinosaurs were around for a long time—at least 167 million years. They first arrived on the scene in the Triassic, 233 million years ago, and they lasted until the Late Cretaceous, around 66 million years ago.

Mesozoic Timeline

EARLY TRIASSIC
252 to 247 million years ago

→

MIDDLE TRIASSIC
247 to 237 million years ago

→

LATE TRIASSIC
237 to 201 million years ago

→

EARLY JURASSIC
201 to 175 million years ago

→

earliest dinosaurs

Most impressive frill *Styracosaurus*

Strongest bite *Tyrannosaurus*

Best head crest *Parasaurolophus*

Most misunderstood
Oviraptor

Longest neck
Mamenchisaurus

MIDDLE JURASSIC
175 to 162
million years ago

LATE JURASSIC
162 to 145
million years ago

EARLY CRETACEOUS
145 to 101
million years ago

LATE CRETACEOUS
101 to 66
million years ago

Sturdiest *Ankylosaurus*

INTRODUCTION
continued

If you're reading this book, you're probably a dinosaur fan. Why do you love dinosaurs?
(There's no wrong answer here!)

For us, we love a good mystery. We'll never know exactly what dinosaurs looked like or how they acted because they're long, long gone and there's no such thing as a time machine.

Dinosaurs fascinated people all over the world long before the word "dinosaur" was invented in 1841. The legendary dragons and serpents of Africa, Asia, Europe, and South America may have been inspired by dinosaur fossils. In Western Australia, the Goolarabooloo and Yawuru peoples recognized that large dinosaur tracks in the rock resembled enormous emu prints. The Zuni people, who have lived in the American Southwest for thousands of years, learned from dinosaur fossils that monstrous animals with huge teeth and sharp claws used to dominate the land before eventually turning into stone. They even figured out that dinosaurs limited our mammalian ancestors to lesser roles long before Darwinian scientists described evolution.

You might think that there's not much left to learn about dinosaurs, since they've been gone for so long. But that couldn't be further from the truth! New dinosaurs are found every week, and each discovery helps improve our understanding of dinosaurs. **That's the beauty of science—we're always learning new things and building on what we know.**

We—Sabrina and Garret—get to talk about all of that new research on our dinosaur podcast *I Know Dino*! We love dinosaurs so much that we had a dinosaur-themed wedding (complete with an animatronic *T. rex* named Duncan, who took lots of photos with us). Afterward, we didn't want to stop talking about dinosaurs, so we started our own show.

We've split this book into six chapters full of entries about different dinosaur species. The dinosaurs appear in order of when they were named. Each entry includes a pronunciation guide to show the most common way to say the dinosaur's name, although there are many correct ways to say certain dinosaur names. Our understanding of what dinosaurs looked and acted like has changed over time, and we explore many of those changes in this book.

Each chapter represents a different period of dinosaur paleontology, and each period featured builds upon the previous one:

- 🐾 **Dinosaur Firsts** (1820s to 1860s): This period covers the first dinosaur finds, such as the first dinosaur to get a scientific name, the first dinosaur found with feathers, and more.
- 🐾 **The Bone Wars** (1870s to 1890s): A notorious time when two rival scientists had a fierce competition over dino discoveries. There was a lot of fallout, but they made dinosaurs famous.
- 🐾 **Exploration Era** (1900s to 1950s): This is when fossil hunters found the first dinosaur eggs, famous predators, and beloved plant-eaters.
- 🐾 **Dinosaur Renaissance** (1960s to 1980s): During this period, people started thinking of dinosaurs as birdlike, warm-blooded, and active.
- 🐾 **Dinosaur Blockbusters** (1990s to early 2000s): A time when major motion pictures kicked off a new gold rush of dinosaur exploration and a revival in dinosaur science.
- 🐾 **The Golden Age** (present day): The period we currently live in! A new dinosaur is discovered almost every week.

It's an exciting time to be a dinosaur fan. Not only is what we know about dinosaurs changing, but also where we find dinosaurs. Most of the earliest named dinosaurs were from Western Europe and North America. But now paleontologists regularly find dinosaurs on all seven continents, including Antarctica!

Our scientific understanding of dinosaurs is constantly improving. This book presents the state of the science today, but it is just a snapshot in time. As long as passionate paleontologists continue finding new bones (and re-examining old bones) our view of dinosaurs will continue to come into sharper focus.

And who knows what they'll find next?

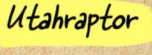

Utahraptor

1

DINOSAUR FIRSTS

==You know the satisfied feeling you get from putting together a jigsaw puzzle? That's what it's like piecing together dinosaur bones. Only, when it comes to dinosaurs, there's no picture on the box to guide you.==

These days, since paleontologists have already found many different kinds of dinosaurs, they aren't starting from scratch with new discoveries. They have a "cheat sheet" that helps them compare new bones to known skeletons. But when dinosaurs were first described in the 1800s, scientists often only had a few bones to work with and had to guess how they fit together. Sometimes all they had to go on was a single tooth!

They didn't always guess right. Spikes found near the dinosaur *Hylaeosaurus*'s shoulder were originally thought to be spines on its back, and then spikes under its belly. Eventually, experts figured out they were shoulder spikes after all—which was exactly where they were when the fossils were first dug up. Turns out, everyone was overthinking it.

Keep reading to learn about more dinosaur firsts from this early period of dinosaur discovery, such as the first dinosaur named, the first dinosaur on display, and the first known feathered dinosaur!

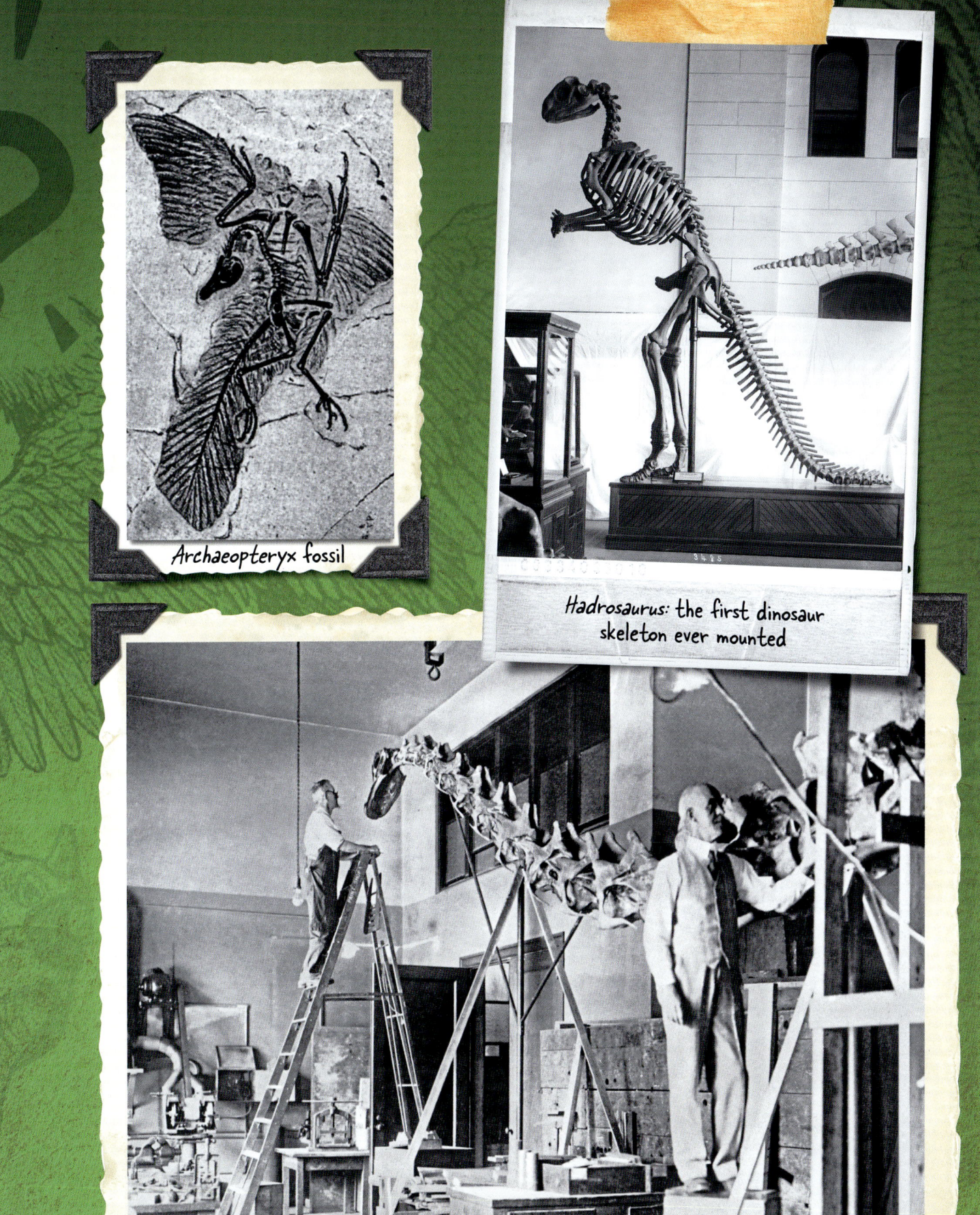

Archaeopteryx fossil

Hadrosaurus: the first dinosaur skeleton ever mounted

The first full dinosaur skeleton discovered in North America

MEGALOSAURUS

The first dinosaur fossil ever described was discovered in 1676. The bone was so incredibly large that people came up with all kinds of stories about where it was from. Some thought it came from an enormous ancient elephant, maybe one that the Romans rode into battle. Later, people thought the bone came from a giant human!

We now know the fossil was probably a *Megalosaurus* leg bone, based on a detailed illustration. Unfortunately for all of us, that bone was lost centuries ago. We'll never know for sure if it was actually from a *Megalosaurus* or some giant Roman elephant after all!

Fast Facts

WHEN IT LIVED: Middle Jurassic (about 166 million years ago)		**WHERE FOSSILS FIRST FOUND:** England
LENGTH: Roughly 20 feet (6 m)	**WHAT IT ATE:** Meat 	
WEIGHT: About 0.8 ton (0.7 t)	**NAMED BY:** William Buckland in 1824	

FIRST IMPRESSIONS

A long, curved tooth standing upright in the middle of a powerful, sturdy jaw: Imagine figuring out what an entire dinosaur looked like just by piecing together a few fossils like this one, or some rib bones and parts of a leg. That's what happened with the mighty *Megalosaurus*, the first dinosaur ever named.

William Buckland, the paleontologist who named *Megalosaurus*, thought this animal was a giant, extinct lizard that could grow to be as long as 60 or 70 feet (18 to 21 m). Sculptures from the 1850s made *Megalosaurus* look like a bear with a long tail dragging behind it. This version also had a small hump around its thick neck.

WHAT WE KNOW NOW

No complete skeletons of *Megalosaurus* have been found yet, but close relatives like *Torvosaurus* have helped scientists understand what *Megalosaurus* looked like. We now know *Megalosaurus* walked on two legs with its tail parallel to the ground. This carnivorous dinosaur also had a long head and a swan-shaped neck.

Today, scientists call the group of dinosaurs that includes *Megalosaurus* theropods. Most theropods were fast, smart predators that walked on two legs and had sharp teeth. But not all theropods were like *Megalosaurus*. Some ate insects and others only ate plants.

Theropods are still around today, but we usually call modern theropod species by another name: birds!

"Leaping Laelaps"!

For many years *Megalosaurus* was a wastebasket taxon, meaning the name *Megalosaurus* was used for many other predatory dinosaurs. In 1869, the paleontologist Edward Drinker Cope drew one of those dinosaurs (briefly known as *Laelaps*) upright on two legs, with its tail dragging on the ground. In 1897, artist Charles R. Knight painted "Leaping Laelaps," which shows one carnivorous dinosaur high off the ground leaping onto another. That painting is a rare early example of a very active dinosaur, when most people were still thinking of them as slow, lumbering beasts.

Knight's 1897 painting

(ig-WAN-oh-don)
"IGUANA TOOTH"

IGUANODON

What has two thumb spikes and is the second dinosaur ever named? *Iguanodon!* We don't really know what *Iguanodon*'s thumb spikes were for, but they may have been used to defend against predators or get food (or maybe to come out on top in thumb wrestling).

Dinner in a Dino

On New Year's Eve 1853, Benjamin Waterhouse Hawkins hosted a dinner party inside an *Iguanodon* statue he created for the Crystal Palace, a glass structure in England that (among other things) showcased the first dinosaur sculptures. He invited 21 guests to celebrate. They ate ham, drank wine, and started singing, "The jolly old beast is not deceased, there's life in him again!"

Iguanodon dinner party

Fast Facts

WHEN IT LIVED:
Early Cretaceous (126 to 122 million years ago)

LENGTH:
Up to about 30 to 36 feet (9 to 11 m)

WEIGHT:
About 5 tons (4.5 t)

WHAT IT ATE:
Plants

NAMED BY:
Gideon Mantell in 1825

WHERE FOSSILS FIRST FOUND:
England

FIRST IMPRESSIONS

The first *Iguanodon* find was just its teeth. Gideon Mantell named the dinosaur, but it's possible his wife Mary Ann Mantell was the one who found it. We're not totally sure who first discovered the fossils, but we do know that Mary beautifully illustrated the strange teeth, which look like giant iguana teeth. This led scientists to think *Iguanodon* was basically a supersize iguana.

Shortly after describing the teeth, Mantell described a more complete skeleton that had a small spike. He suggested the spike was a horn on its nose, like the one some iguanas have!

WHAT WE KNOW NOW

In 1878, not long after _Iguanodon_ was named, coal mine workers found a bone bed—a rock layer full of bones. This bone bed was packed with over 30 _Iguanodon_ skeletons in what was once a lake. These _Iguanodon_ all died together, possibly from drowning or because they inhaled poisonous gases. Shortly after they passed away, their bodies were buried and fossilized at the bottom of the lake.

It was a tragedy for them, but great for scientists. Some of the _Iguanodon_ fossils even had impressions that showed the texture of their skin!

Because so many _Iguanodon_ bones have been found, we now know the dinosaur wasn't like a giant iguana. _Iguanodon_'s long tail was stiff and helped it balance. It also had a beak and hooflike hands, with three of its fingers stuck close together. The hooflike hands could help the dinosaur walk on all fours, though it could also walk on two legs when it needed to reach for food.

IGUANODON was named 16 years before the word "dinosaur" was invented.

HADROSAURUS

Hadrosaurus was the first dinosaur skeleton regular members of the public ever got to see, but it had the wrong head! Its bones were found in 1838 in Haddonfield, New Jersey, U.S.A. The skull was missing, but there were enough fossils to put together the body— and scientists made their best guess about the head. So in 1868, the Academy of Natural Sciences at Drexel University unveiled a *Hadrosaurus* skeleton with the head of an iguana.

Fast Facts

WHEN IT LIVED: Late Cretaceous (80 to 78 million years ago)

LENGTH:	NAMED BY:	WHERE FOSSILS FIRST FOUND:
About 26 feet (8 m)	Joseph Leidy in 1858	New Jersey, U.S.A.
WEIGHT: Roughly 2 to 4 tons (2 to 4 t)	**WHAT IT ATE:** Plants	

FIRST IMPRESSIONS

When scientists first reconstructed *Hadrosaurus,* everyone thought it stood like a kangaroo: upright on two legs, dragging its tail on the floor. Because no one had found a skull, and the body had some similarities to an iguana, scientists guessed that its head looked similar to an iguana's head. They also thought that *Hadrosaurus* and its relatives lived in the water and ate soft plants.

WHAT WE KNOW *NOW*

Discovering other types of hadrosaurs helped paleontologists figure out what *Hadrosaurus* (probably!) looked like. Fossil hunters have found many skeletons, including skulls, of one of its relatives: *Edmontosaurus*.

Because of these discoveries, we know *Hadrosaurus* was a duck-billed dinosaur.

But unlike a duck, *Hadrosaurus* had hundreds of teeth stacked together to form an almost flat surface. This made it super easy to grind down plants.

Hadrosaurus and its relatives also looked and acted more like horses than ducks! They had long heads like a horse, ate a lot of plants, were good runners (large tail muscles helped lift their legs), and would have been large enough to ride—if you could tame one.

DINOSAUR MUMMIES

How does a dinosaur become a fossil? What we call fossils are usually the preserved remains of animals and plants that can survive in rock for millions of years. But how did those remains get inside the rock in the first place?

Imagine a dinosaur got stuck in the mud and died in a lake. If everything went just right (for us, not for the poor dinosaur), it could become a fossil.

Dirt would cover the dinosaur remains, protecting them from scavengers and weather. Over time, the skin and other soft tissues would often rot away while minerals slowly filled in small spaces in the bones. Eventually, the bones would become embedded in the rock—a fossil! Then, if we're lucky, someone finds the fossilized bones and digs them up.

But how does a dinosaur become a mummy? Some dinosaurs—especially hadrosaurs—have been found still covered in skin. We call them "mummies."

Dino mummies are an especially strange type of fossil. One possibility is that they were created in a process called desiccation and deflation. Maybe a carnivore bit holes in the skin of a dinosaur to eat the tasty insides but left behind the tough, less meaty parts. The holes in the skin allowed the body to dry out ("desiccate"). Then the skin collapsed ("deflated") onto the bones before the dino was buried. Finally, this tough dry skin slowly turned into rock. Let's meet a few dino mummies!

DAKOTA THE EDMONTOSAURUS

Dakota is a nearly complete *Edmontosaurus* (only the head, tail tip, and left arm are missing). About half of Dakota is covered in skin. Because the fossil has a lot of iron in it, the skin glitters!

There are tooth and claw marks on the skin, which means there was time after Dakota died for animals to scavenge and eat it. Dakota helps show us that mummified dinosaurs didn't have to be buried quickly after death in order to mummify.

Dakota's right hand, with lots of skin still covering the bones

LEONARDO THE BRACHYLOPHOSAURUS

One of the most famous dinosaur mummies is Leonardo, a *Brachylophosaurus.*

Leonardo was about 22 feet (7 m) long and weighed roughly two tons (2 t). But that's not what's unusual: Almost all (90 percent) of Leonardo is covered in skin!

Inside Leonardo's gut were ferns, conifers, magnolias, and pollen from more than 40 different plants. Poor Leonardo also had small, needlelike worm parasites in its stomach.

You can see the thick muscles in Leonardo's neck!

ARCHAEOPTERYX

Archaeopteryx was a birdlike dinosaur, complete with a beak, feathers, and wings. But watch out—unlike the mouths of modern birds, its mouth was full of sharp teeth!

Considering, though, that *Archaeopteryx* was about the size of a crow, it's likely its teeth were used mostly for catching bugs.

Fast Facts

WHEN IT LIVED: Late Jurassic (about 150 million years ago)

LENGTH:
About 1.7 feet (0.5 m)

WHAT IT ATE:
Meat/Insects

WEIGHT:
Up to 2 pounds (0.9 kg)

NAMED BY:
Hermann von Meyer in 1861

WHERE FOSSILS FIRST FOUND:
Germany

FIRST IMPRESSIONS

It's a bird! It's a plane! It's a ... headless dinosaur?

Archaeopteryx was named for a single long, dark, fossilized feather. For a couple of years, that was the only thing documented about it.

Fortunately, in 1863, scientists announced a more complete skeleton: the London specimen. It included bones from most of the *Archaeopteryx*'s body. More importantly, there were feathers from its large wings and tail. The name "ancient wing" proved correct, and experts started talking more about the connection between dinosaurs and birds.

Like many dinosaur firsts, however, the London specimen was missing a head. Scientists didn't want to guess what the head looked like, so in 1866, an artist drew a flying headless *Archaeopteryx*.

Birds today do not have teeth, but some have tongues **COVERED IN LONG SPIKES!**

WHAT WE KNOW NOW

Since the 1860s, 12 *Archaeopteryx* skeletons have been discovered. The best example is known as the Berlin specimen. In addition to a mouth full of small teeth, nearly every bone in the dinosaur's body is preserved in a lifelike pose.

Small claws on the ends of its fingers stuck out from the front of its wings. It's possible *Archaeopteryx* used its claws to climb trees just as some baby birds do today.

A long tail covered in feathers made it too difficult for *Archaeopteryx* to fly long distances. But it could fly for at least short bursts of time.

In 2005, paleontologists described the Thermopolis specimen, which shows evidence that *Archaeopteryx* molted (or shed its feathers). We learned from its feet that unlike modern birds that can perch in tree branches, *Archaeopteryx* didn't have a backward-facing toe. That tells us that *Archaeopteryx* wouldn't have been able to hold on to a branch; it might have spent more time on the ground or clung to the trunks of trees.

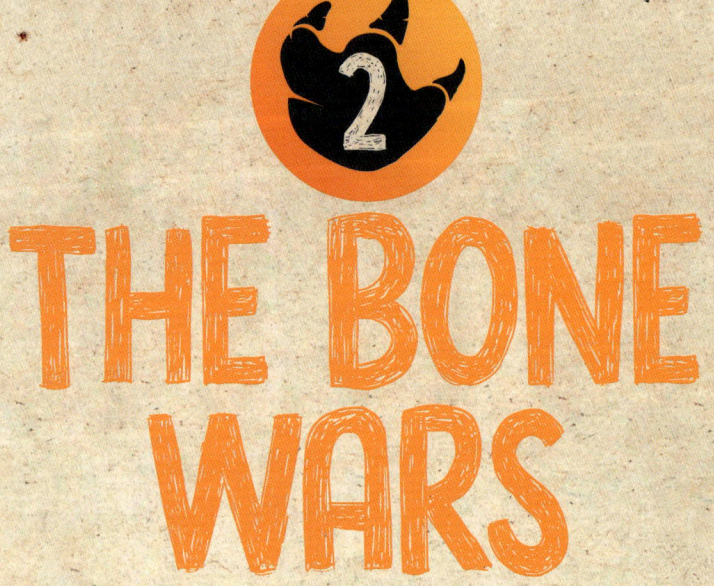

THE BONE WARS

Explosions, spies, and shootouts: It sounds like the plot of a thriller, but it all happened during the Bone Wars! This real-life conflict made "dinosaur" a household word.

Between the 1870s and 1890s, two rival paleontologists, Othniel Charles Marsh and Edward Drinker Cope, fiercely competed to find and name the most dinosaur species. They went so far as to bribe, steal, and destroy bones to prevent each other from winning.

Before the Bone Wars, dinosaurs were not that popular. Only nine dinosaurs had been named in the United States, where Marsh and Cope lived and worked, and they were mostly based on just teeth and fragments of skeletons. Marsh and Cope changed all that and ended up naming over 130 species of dinosaurs. However, in their rush, Marsh and Cope identified a lot of dinosaurs that turned out to be other animals or duplicates of already known dinosaurs. Today only 32 of their dinosaur names are still used.

Some of the dinosaur species named during the Bone Wars are among the most well-known today, including *Brontosaurus*, *Stegosaurus*, *Triceratops*, and many others.

What we know about these Bone Wars dinosaurs has changed a lot since the 1800s. To explore what's new since the wild days of Marsh and Cope, we'll cover three famous dinosaurs: *Stegosaurus*, *Diplodocus*, and *Triceratops*.

Prof O. C. Marsh
MAULL & C°.   LONDON.
1866.

Left:
O. C. Marsh described almost 500 animal species (including more than 80 dinosaurs)!

Right:
Edward Drinker Cope described more than 1,000 animal species (including more than 50 dinosaurs)!

Othniel Charles Marsh

All set to hunt for dinosaurs

(STEG-oh-SORE-us)
"ROOF LIZARD"

STEGOSAURUS

These days, *Stegosaurus* is one of the most recognizable dinosaurs. But before anyone had published a scientific illustration of the animal, artists came up with their own ideas about what it looked like. In 1884, seven years before Marsh published his *Stegosaurus* skeleton, the illustrator Auguste Jobin showed *Stegosaurus* looking pretty much like Godzilla (decades before the creation of the character)! Jobin's *Stegosaurus* stood on two legs, with its tail dragging behind it. Sharp spikes ran down in rows on its back and tail. Fierce, definitely! But as we know today, not very accurate.

Fast Facts

WHEN IT LIVED: Late Jurassic (155 to 150 million years ago)		
LENGTH: Up to 25 feet (7.5 m)	**WEIGHT:** Up to 6 tons (5 t)	**WHERE FOSSILS FIRST FOUND:** Colorado, U.S.A.
NAMED BY: Othniel Charles Marsh in 1877	**WHAT IT ATE:** Plants	

FIRST IMPRESSIONS

As a Bone Wars dinosaur, *Stegosaurus* was named in a hurry—before its skeleton was even removed from the rock where it was preserved. When he named *Stegosaurus*, Othniel Charles Marsh had only identified part of the tail and part of one of the plates from its back.

Marsh thought that *Stegosaurus* spent most of its time in water. He also suggested that *Stegosaurus's* famous tall plates were armor that lay flat on its body, like the shell of a turtle.

The Thagomizer

At the tip of its tail, *Stegosaurus* had a fearsome weapon: four large spikes ready to skewer any threatening predator. The name of this weapon? The thagomizer.

The name comes from a surprising source: a comic strip from 1982 called "The Far Side." In the comic, a caveman points to a spiky *Stegosaurus* tail and calls it "thagomizer ... after the late Thag Simmons" (his fictitious friend). Many paleontologists loved the joke and have used the term "thagomizer" in presentations and publications since. Art and science often build off each other.

WHAT WE KNOW NOW

Ten years after finding the first *Stegosaurus*, Marsh found a nearly complete skeleton. This included 17 back plates.

Since then, paleontologists have found fossils from more than a hundred *Stegosaurus* individuals. Now we think the large plates on the dinosaur's back formed two rows with an alternating pattern. *Stegosaurus* would have held its spiked tail, or thagomizer, high off the ground, ready to defend itself at a moment's notice.

Some *Stegosaurus* and *Allosaurus* fossils show they sometimes fought each other. In one case, it looks like *Stegosaurus* used its thagomizer to defend itself.

Some of *Stegosaurus*'s bony back plates were taller than three feet (1 m)! When *Stegosaurus* was alive, its plates may have been even bigger. A horn sheath might have extended beyond the edges of the bone.

(dih-PLOD-uh-kus)
"DOUBLE BEAM"

DIPLODOCUS

Diplodocus **had a long enough neck** that it could stand on the ground outside your house, snake its head through a second-story window, and steal the lunch off your plate from across the room. But the tail of *Diplodocus* was the real showstopper: It was twice as long as its neck!

Fast Facts

WHEN IT LIVED: Late Jurassic (about 154 to 152 million years ago)

LENGTH: About 85 feet (26 m)

WEIGHT: About 14 tons (13 t)

WHAT IT ATE: Plants

WHERE FOSSILS FIRST FOUND: Colorado, U.S.A.

NAMED BY: Othniel Charles Marsh in 1878

FIRST IMPRESSIONS

The first complete sauropod (long-necked dinosaur) skull found was from *Diplodocus* or a close relative. The skull was surprisingly tiny, making up less than one percent of the dino's body size. It also had fragile, peglike teeth that showed the dinosaur ate plants.

Originally, paleontologists thought *Diplodocus* dragged its tail on the ground and could barely lift its head much higher. They also assumed this dinosaur's tail was about the same length as its neck.

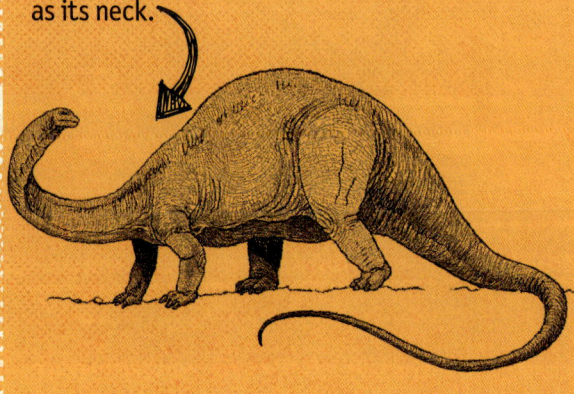

Cetiosaurus

Whale Lizards

The first sauropod bones were so large scientists thought they could only come from a whalelike creature. That's why the first sauropod was named *Cetiosaurus*, or "whale lizard."

For years, paleontologists thought that because sauropods were so heavy, the only way they could survive was with water supporting their bodies.

Sauropods like **DIPLODOCUS** had claws on their back feet that may have been specialized for digging nests.

WHAT WE KNOW NOW

Diplodocus was the first sauropod to be displayed in Europe. King Edward VII of England requested that Andrew Carnegie, who had a growing collection of dinosaur bones, send him a dinosaur of his own. Carnegie delivered a replica of *Diplodocus* nicknamed "Dippy." Dippy made its debut at the Natural History Museum in London in 1905 and stayed there in various spaces for over a century.

More than 130 *Diplodocus* skeletons have been found since the dinosaur was named in the 1800s, and this new research led to updates to Dippy. In the 1960s the dinosaur's head was lifted off the ground, and in 1993 the tail was twisted to the side to show off its flexibility.

But what did *Diplodocus* use its tail for? Maybe it cracked the tail like a whip, swatted at predators, or used it to communicate. It's still up for debate.

TRICERATOPS

Another all-star dinosaur discovery from the Bone Wars era, *Triceratops* is one of the most front-heavy dinosaurs, with a superlarge skull.

One skull found in South Dakota, for example, is 8.6 feet (2.6 m) long and weighs over 1,500 pounds (700 kg)!

Fast Facts

WHEN IT LIVED: Late Cretaceous (about 68 to 66 million years ago)		**WHERE FOSSILS FIRST FOUND:** Colorado, U.S.A.
LENGTH: Up to 26 feet (8 m)	**WHAT IT ATE:** Plants	
WEIGHT: Up to 11 tons (10 t)	**NAMED BY:** Othniel Charles Marsh in 1889	

FIRST IMPRESSIONS

The first *Triceratops* fossils found were a pair of long, pointy horns and a piece of skull connecting them. Othniel Charles Marsh thought they belonged to a bison because bison have long horns above their eyes. Eventually, more complete *Triceratops* skulls and skeletons were found. That helped Marsh figure out that those first horns were from a dinosaur.

Rushing to name as many dinosaurs as possible in order to defeat his rival Marsh, Edward Cope came up with two extra names for fossils that are actually probably just *Triceratops*: *Agathaumas* and *Polyonax*.

Triceratops was way bigger than a bison—about five times its size!

WHAT WE KNOW NOW

To hold up that giant head, *Triceratops* had a strong short neck and a frill to cover it. The frill was a bony structure behind its horns. It had three horns: one on its snout, like a rhinoceros, and a pair of horns above its eyes that could be more than three feet (1 m) long.

In 2022, paleontologists studied keratin (a material that makes up fingernails, hair, and feathers, and covers animal horns and claws) from some of *Triceratops*'s distant relatives. They found that the keratin covering *Triceratops*'s brow horns may have made its horns much bigger, possibly almost five feet (about 1.5 m) long!

A *Triceratops* battle

Triceratops vs. Triceratops

Just because *Triceratops* was a herbivore doesn't mean the dinosaurs were friendly. *Triceratops* probably fought each other using their horns. Fossil hunters have found more than 50 *Triceratops* skulls, which is a lot for a dinosaur. Some skulls have holes that match the shape and size of a *Triceratops* horn.

COOL CERATOPSIDS

Long as a car or short as a mailbox, solid as a rock or full of holes like Swiss cheese, dinosaur frills came in all shapes and sizes. They would have been super helpful, too, for impressing potential mates, scaring off rivals, defending against predators, and more.

Though all ceratopsids had beaks for cropping plants, they're probably more famous for their frills. No dinosaur could rock a frill better than a ceratopsid (like *Triceratops*)! These frilled dinosaurs can be divided into two groups: centrosaurines and chasmosaurines.

Centrosaurines

You can recognize centrosaurines by the impressive horn on their nose, along with generally shorter frills and shorter horns above their eyes than chasmosaurines.

Styracosaurus: This dinosaur's frill had four to six long spikes sticking out. Many skulls have been found, and they show that individual frills looked slightly different from each other. For example, some frills had hooks and knobs on them.

Einiosaurus: This dinosaur is known for the horn on its nose with a strong forward curve. It also had two large spikes that stuck out from the edge of its frill.

Chasmosaurines

Chasmosaurines (like *Triceratops*) are generally known for having larger frills and smaller horns on their nose than centrosaurines (although not always).

Regaliceratops: Its name means "royal horned face," and it refers to the crown-like appearance of the frill on its head. Triangular horns lined the edge of the frill, and the frill itself had distinct, rounded decorations.

Kosmoceratops: This dinosaur had one of the fanciest frills, with hooklike bony extensions bending over the top.

3

EXPLORATION ERA

Scorching deserts. Wicked dust storms. Secrets hidden deep within the rocks for millions of years. It was the dawn of the 1900s—a thrilling, extraordinary time. Fossil hunters could use cameras, cars, and even camels to explore new horizons and discover fantastical dinosaurs stranger than anyone had ever imagined.

Two of the most famous fossil hunters were Barnum Brown and Roy Chapman Andrews. Barnum Brown was so good at finding fossils (he discovered and dug up the first *T. rex* skeleton!) that his nickname was Mr. Bones.

Roy Chapman Andrews had his own claims to fame. He indirectly inspired the character Indiana Jones and narrowly escaped death many times. Once, bandits on horseback chased him while he was driving his car. Another time a wounded whale charged his boat. Wild dogs almost ate Andrews and his wife, and pit vipers drove him and his team away from their campsite.

The Exploration Era also included the first woman to both discover and describe a dinosaur. In 1911, paleontologist Mignon Talbot named *Podokesaurus* (now the state dinosaur of Massachusetts).

These explorers found the first dinosaur eggs, the biggest, most famous predators, and some of the most beloved plant-eaters.

Mignon Talbot

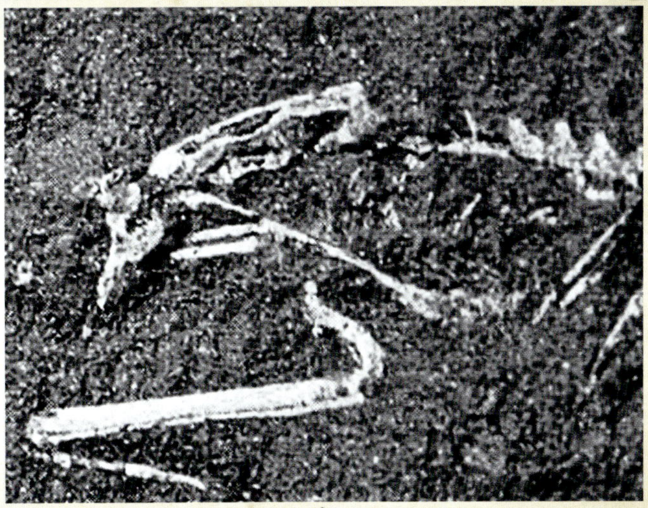

Pumped to have found *Podokesaurus*

Roy Chapman Andrews and crew hard at work in the Gobi desert, 1928

(BRACK-ee-oh-SORE-us)
"ARM LIZARD"

BRACHIOSAURUS

Peeking between the leaves of a tall, bushy-looking ginkgo tree was a dinosaur with a long neck and small head: a *Brachiosaurus*. As it kept its neck upright to eat the leaves off the tree, its head would have been about 36 feet (11 m) above the ground. That's taller than a two-story house!

Fast Facts

WHEN IT LIVED: Late Jurassic (about 154 to 150 million years ago)

LENGTH: About 72 feet (22 m)

WHAT IT ATE: Plants

WEIGHT: At least 31 tons (28 t)

NAMED BY: Elmer Riggs in 1903

WHERE FOSSILS FIRST FOUND: Colorado, U.S.A.

FIRST IMPRESSIONS

Brachiosaurus's **head really stood out.** It had a big bump on the top—as if someone had hit it really hard with a giant hammer.

For a long time, paleontologists thought *Brachiosaurus* had nostrils on the top of its head, and that they worked like a snorkel. With that snorkel, *Brachiosaurus* could walk to the bottom of a deep lake, even keeping its eyes underwater, and still breathe air. (The famous paleoartist Zdeněk Burian painted a pair of *Brachiosaurus* completely in water.)

Brachiosaurus may look like a giraffe, but a close relative has the actual name "titanic giraffe": *Giraffatitan*.

Like a giraffe, **BRACHIOSAURUS'S** front legs were longer than its back legs.

WHAT WE KNOW NOW

In reality, *Brachiosaurus* probably spent nearly all its time on land. In 2001 Lawrence Witmer studied the nostrils of dinosaurs and other animals. By comparing crocodiles, lizards, turtles, birds, and mammals to dinosaurs, he found that dinosaurs in general would have had nostrils on the front of their snouts.

Having nostrils on the front of its snout instead of the top of its head would have helped *Brachiosaurus* breathe better. Not quite as good for snorkeling through a lake, though!

(tye-RAN-oh-SORE-us)
"TYRANT LIZARD"

TYRANNOSAURUS

You might think if you arm-wrestled *Tyrannosaurus,* you'd win. After all, compared to its large body and massive skull, *Tyrannosaurus* had puny arms. But don't count your chickens (or your tyrannosaurs) before they hatch. *Tyrannosaurus* had biceps 3.5 times as powerful as ours. That means it could have easily curled about 145 pounds (66 kg) with just one of its arms.

And don't forget: While wrestling, you'd have to avoid its teeth. They were shaped like bananas, which sounds cute, but they could crush bone. Paleontologist Karen Chin and her team once found pieces of bone in a fossilized poop (also known as a coprolite). It's hard to know for sure, but based on the hefty size of the turd, the scientists think a *Tyrannosaurus* individual made this number two. It probably ate some bone that it didn't fully digest.

Tyrannosaurus was one of the last dinosaurs to ever live, but it's been extinct for over 65 million years. We should feel pretty lucky that we don't have to worry about arm wrestling these brawny dinosaurs or avoiding their chompers.

FIRST IMPRESSIONS

From the beginning, scientists knew *Tyrannosaurus* was large and powerful. Newspaper articles even called it the "last of the great reptiles and king of them all."

But as is the case with many dinosaurs, when *Tyrannosaurus* was first found, some of its bones were missing. The first *Tyrannosaurus* skeletons had no hands. So when researchers were getting *Tyrannosaurus* ready for display at the American Museum of Natural History in New York, they gave the dinosaur three fingers, like its much older relative *Allosaurus.* Walt Disney did the same in his 1940 movie *Fantasia.* Even though scientists had some evidence by then that *Tyrannosaurus* only had two fingers, Disney insisted they animate the dinosaur with three fingers because he thought it looked better.

Researchers also made *Tyrannosaurus* look like a "living tripod," with its tail dragging, almost like a third leg.

Fast Facts

WHEN IT LIVED: Late Cretaceous (about 68 to 66 million years ago)

LENGTH: Up to about 42 feet (13 m)	**WHAT IT ATE:** Meat
WEIGHT: Up to 10 tons (9 t)	**NAMED BY:** Henry Fairfield Osborn in 1905

WHERE FOSSILS FIRST FOUND: Wyoming, U.S.A.

turn the page for more on *Tyrannosaurus* ➡

WHAT WE KNOW NOW

We now know *Tyrannosaurus* had only two fingers on each hand. In 1988, an amateur fossil hunter found a new *Tyrannosaurus* skeleton that included the dinosaur's arms and hands.

What paleontologists are still trying to figure out is how fluffy *Tyrannosaurus* was, and whether or not it had lips covering its teeth. Even if it did, who would want to pucker up for that ferocious dinosaur?

Some *Tyrannosaurus* relatives have been found with feathers. *Tyrannosaurus* might have had feathers, too, or at least their babies did. No *Tyrannosaurus* skeletons have been found with evidence of feathers. However, they have been found with scales.

As for the lips, the debate is all about the teeth. Smile, and pull your lips back. Try to keep your teeth out in the open for a few seconds. Can you tell your teeth feel drier? Your lips protect your teeth by keeping them hydrated.

Tyrannosaurus may have had a similar setup. In 2023, paleontologists analyzed the teeth of *Daspletosaurus*, a *Tyrannosaurus* relative, and an alligator. Alligators don't have lips, and they found the alligator had more wear and tear on its teeth than *Daspletosaurus*. That may mean tyrannosaurs and other theropod dinosaurs had lips like modern lizards to protect their teeth.

TYRANNOSAURUS was endothermic (warm-blooded) like us.

I see you!

Rexy Vision

In the 1993 movie *Jurassic Park*, what saved the characters from Rexy the *T. rex* was the fact that she couldn't see them if they stood perfectly still. But in real life, *Tyrannosaurus* had excellent vision. *Tyrannosaurus* had the largest eyes of any animal ever to walk the planet and could probably see better than a hawk!

And if *Tyrannosaurus* couldn't see you, it could certainly smell you (even if you recently showered). That's because this dinosaur had a large olfactory bulb in its brain, used to process smells.

When it came to food, *Tyrannosaurus* was probably a hunter and a scavenger. Its ability to smell would have helped it track prey much like a wolf can, and find carcasses to eat as successfully as a turkey vulture.

ANKYLOSAURUS

How could anyone or anything possibly survive a chomp from *T. rex,* the animal with the strongest bite ever to walk on land? Amazingly, *Ankylosaurus* could!

Fortunately for *Ankylosaurus*, it was built like a tank with the armor to defend against *Tyrannosaurus*. Its skin was embedded with more than a hundred pieces of bony armor called osteoderms.

Fast Facts

WHEN IT LIVED: Late Cretaceous (about 68 to 66 million years ago)

LENGTH: About 26 feet (8 m)

WHAT IT ATE: Plants

WEIGHT: About 9 tons (8 t)

NAMED BY: Barnum Brown in 1908

WHERE FOSSILS FIRST FOUND: Montana, U.S.A.

FIRST IMPRESSIONS

When Barnum Brown, who named *Ankylosaurus*, found the first *Ankylosaurus* fossils, he noticed similarities to *Stegosaurus*. That helped him fill in a lot of the missing pieces with information he knew from *Stegosaurus*.

He thought *Ankylosaurus* had a back arched in a semicircle. There was no end of the tail, so he gave it a simple tail tip (no thagomizer or club). Brown found a lot of osteoderms, and he figured that they were tightly packed together, almost like a tortoise shell. (Some *Ankylosaurus* osteoderms were found with the first *T. rex* skeleton, and for a while scientists thought *T. rex* also had armor.)

If *Ankylosaurus* had had long legs, it would have exposed its soft underbelly.

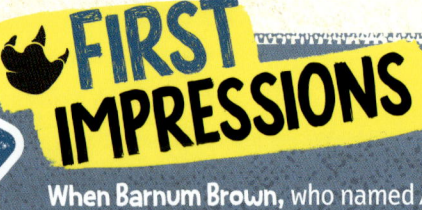

WHAT WE KNOW NOW

Thanks to more complete finds (see *Borealopelta*) and research by experts like **Victoria Arbour,** we have a much better idea now about how *Ankylosaurus* looked. Its legs were shorter than *Stegosaurus*'s, and it held its tail off the ground.

Other than the neck (which had a pair of rigid half rings of armor), *Ankylosaurus*'s osteoderms were more spaced out, giving it a little flexibility. But the biggest change was the discovery in 1910 of its impressive tail club.

A Mural as Big as a Dinosaur

You can see *Ankylosaurus* calmly grazing, despite a ferocious *T. rex* looming over it, in Rudolph Zallinger's 110-foot (33.5-m) mural masterpiece "The Age of Reptiles" at the Yale Peabody Museum of Natural History. The giant painting took Zallinger five years to create, and he completed it in 1947. Though now outdated, this work of art greatly influenced how everyone saw dinosaurs for decades. Even today, some dinosaur toys are based on this painting.

"The Age of Reptiles"

BIG WEAPONS AREN'T JUST FOR PREDATORS

Just because herbivores eat plants, it doesn't mean they can't be ferocious. After all, hippos and elephants are just as dangerous as lions (if not more so).

Many plant-eating dinosaurs had sharp horns, battering-ram heads, powerful tails, or even clubs to protect themselves. (Carnivorous dinosaurs mostly relied on sharp teeth and claws—but the herbivorous *Therizinosaurus* had claws that put every carnivore to shame— see page 60.)

Although animals don't usually have tail weapons, dinosaurs were an exception: Many had a mixture of impressive head and tail weaponry.

Some of these weapons were used for more than defense. One *Zuul* skeleton was injured near its hips. Scientists think another jealous *Zuul* backed up to it and traded blows. Paleontologists have found similar evidence with *Pachycephalosaurus* domes and *Triceratops* horns.

HEADS

Pachycephalosaurus ("thick-headed lizard") had a large dome of bone on top of its head for ramming into other dinosaurs. Some pachycephalosaurs also had horns sticking out from the back of their heads. It's possible they flung their heads backward into each other, in the most awkward-looking battles.

TAILS

Many sauropods, like *Diplodocus*, had extremely long tails—even longer than most dinosaurs! The tails by themselves may have been useful weapons. The small sauropod *Shunosaurus* was only about as long as *Ankylosaurus* and probably weighed less. But like *Ankylosaurus*, *Shunosaurus* had a club on its tail that it could use to defend itself against predators.

TAILS

The ankylosaur *Zuul*'s tail was so fierce that scientists gave this dinosaur the species name *crurivastator* ("destroyer of shins"). *Ankylosaurus* had a similar tail club, but *Anodontosaurus* had the most dramatic ankylosaur tail found so far. Its tail club measured nearly two feet (60 cm) wide and was pointed on the sides to make it even more menacing. All of these ankylosaurs could swing their tail clubs hard enough to shatter the bones of an attacking predator.

HEADS

Ceratopsians ("horned faces") had a wide variety of horns to protect themselves (see "Cool Ceratopsids" on page 30). Some, like *Centrosaurus*, had a single long horn on their nose like a rhino that could easily poke a hole in an attacking predator. Others, like *Diabloceratops*, had a long pair of horns above their eyes and a second pair on top of their frill. Maybe they showed off their horns to potential mates or used them to compete with rivals, similar to the way deer lock their antlers together.

SPINOSAURUS

Think about an animal that looks like a cross between a crocodile and a sailfish. Then imagine it much, much bigger! This is *Spinosaurus:* a fierce predatory dinosaur. *Spinosaurus* is one of the largest known carnivorous dinosaurs to have lived.

The long, narrow head of *Spinosaurus,* full of cone-shaped teeth, was perfect for grabbing slippery fish. Its hands had large claws. The tail looked like a paddle. But strangest of all was the massive sail on its back, formed by tall spines connected by thin skin.

What's not yet clear about *Spinosaurus* is how much time it spent in the water. This central mystery is still an open question—read on to decide what you think!

Fast Facts

WHEN IT LIVED: Late Cretaceous (99 to 93.5 million years ago)

LENGTH: About 46 feet (14 m)	**NAMED BY:** Ernst Stromer in 1915	**WHERE FOSSILS FIRST FOUND:** Egypt
WEIGHT: About 8 tons (7 t)	**WHAT IT ATE:** Fish 	

FIRST IMPRESSIONS

At first, *Spinosaurus* seemed somewhat similar to *T. rex.* Scientists figured it was tall, walked on two legs, had short arms, and dragged its tail. They also knew it had a sail on its back (so no, *Spinosaurus* and *Tyrannosaurus* were never thought to be twins).

Over time, paleontologists changed their minds and thought *Spinosaurus* had a more horizontal posture: It kept its long head more in line with its tail. You can see that version of *Spinosaurus* in the movie *Jurassic Park III.*

SPINOSAURUS bones are rare, but its teeth are much more common because they constantly grew new teeth.

Nizar Ibrahim

Riddle Me This

In the part of Egypt where *Spinosaurus* was originally found, scientists have learned that a wide variety of humongous predatory dinosaurs lived alongside one another. Why?

Scientist Ernst Stromer noticed this curious fact about the big carnivorous dinosaurs. So this mystery is known as Stromer's Riddle. How would there have been enough food for all of them to eat?

Years later, in 2014, paleontologist and National Geographic Explorer Nizar Ibrahim and his team described a new *Spinosaurus*, which they found in Morocco. In this new setting, researchers also found mollusks, sea urchins, and marine animals such as coelacanths and lungfish.

This finding led to the thinking that *Spinosaurus* probably ate fish, which would mean it didn't always have to compete for food with the other predators on land.

However, that doesn't mean *Spinosaurus* didn't eat other animals like pterosaurs or iguanodonts, if given the chance. Dinosaurs, like most animals, would never have passed up an easy meal.

turn the page for more on *Spinosaurus* ➡

WHAT WE KNOW NOW

Scientists are still actively studying *Spinosaurus,* and our understanding of this animal is always changing as discoveries are made. In 2014, paleontologist Nizar Ibrahim and his team announced that *Spinosaurus* was semiaquatic. They made a number of observations that supported this idea, including:

- *Spinosaurus* could detect movement in the water with its snout.
- Its teeth were built for catching fish.
- It had small nostrils high on its face to make it easy to breathe while its head was in the water.
- The back legs were shorter than scientists previously thought, similar to early whales and other mammals that use their legs to move in water.
- It had flat feet that may have been webbed, to help move in the water (and stand on soft wet mud).
- Its bone density was much greater than other theropods, such as *T. rex,* to help it stay underwater while swimming.

In 2020, Ibrahim and his team published another outstanding discovery: *Spinosaurus* had a long, flat, paddle-like tail, which, according to them, would have been used for swimming.

The next year, a different team of researchers argued that *Spinosaurus* was more of a wader than a specialized predator in the water, usually fishing on shore.

Then in 2022, two studies came out: One described how *Spinosaurus* had dense bones that would have helped it dive underwater. The other study found *Spinosaurus* was unstable in water and could have walked well on two legs on land.

The debate continues.

Original *Spinosaurus* fossils

Lost Holotype

The original fossils, known as the holotype, of *Spinosaurus* that Ernst Stromer found were destroyed during World War II when the United Kingdom's Royal Air Force dropped more than 200 bombs and set fire to Munich, Germany.

SPINOSAURUS couldn't fold its sail down. The sail was part of the bones of its spine.

PARASAUROLOPHUS

What noises did dinosaurs make? Some may have tweeted like a songbird, growled like an alligator, or boomed like an emu. For most dinosaurs, we will never know the answer to this question. But we have a theory about *Parasaurolophus*, which had a large hollow crest on its head that looked a little like a trombone.

Fast Facts

WHEN IT LIVED: Late Cretaceous (about 76 to 73 million years ago)

LENGTH: About 30 feet (9 m)	**WHAT IT ATE:** Plants
WEIGHT: About 6 tons (5 t)	**NAMED BY:** William Parks in 1922

WHERE FOSSILS FIRST FOUND: Alberta, Canada

FIRST IMPRESSIONS

When *Parasaurolophus* was first named, paleontologists thought it had skin that started on its head crest and connected to the neck. How frilling!

Scientists also had ideas about how *Parasaurolophus* used its crest. They suggested that the crest

🐾 was full of smell receptors to sniff out tasty treats;

🐾 stored air like a built-in scuba tank;

🐾 helped it battle other *Parasaurolophus*;

🐾 let other *Parasaurolophus* know where it ranked, socially (like a crown!); and

🐾 made sounds.

The crests of ***PARASAUROLOPHUS*** came in slightly different shapes and sizes.

In 2020, paleontologists closely studied the original *Parasaurolophus* skeleton (the one that scientists thought had a frill). They found that the poor dinosaur was badly injured and probably walked with a limp. It had likely been hit by something, which led to extra bone growth at the exact spot where scientists had thought a frill was attached. But instead of having a frill or sail, *Parasaurolophus* probably just had a big bump on its back.

In the 1990s, researchers took powerful x-rays of a *Parasaurolophus* skull and modeled its sound on a computer. They simulated air flowing in through the nose and up through the crest and found that *Parasaurolophus* could use its crest to make several noises—mostly low rumbling sounds. We can't be sure if they were right, but we know that low sounds are especially useful because they carry across longer distances, allowing animals to communicate with family and friends from far away.

MAJESTIC CRESTS

Parasaurolophus wasn't the only hadrosaur with a fancy head. Many of its relatives had crests, too. They couldn't all make sounds, though—some crests were completely solid!

Lambeosaurus

Saurolophus

Velafrons

Tsintaosaurus

Amurosaurus

Corythosaurus

PSITTACOSAURUS

If you could have a pet dinosaur, *Psittacosaurus* would be a pretty good choice! This early ceratopsian was fairly small (for a dinosaur).

There were multiple species of *Psittacosaurus*, but only one had a frill. However, all species of *Psittacosaurus* were covered in scales, and they all had quills sticking out from the top of their tails (like an upside-down broom).

Fast Facts

WHEN IT LIVED: Early Cretaceous (about 126 to 101 million years ago)		**WHERE FOSSILS FIRST FOUND:** Mongolia
LENGTH: About 6 feet (1.8 meters)	**WHAT IT ATE:**  Plants	
WEIGHT: Up to 44 pounds (20 kg)	**NAMED BY:** Henry Fairfield Osborn in 1923	

FIRST IMPRESSIONS

Although the first *Psittacosaurus* fossils found were of a nearly complete skeleton, when researchers named the dinosaur, they still didn't know exactly what it looked like. That's because they described the dinosaur while its bones were still stuck in the rock where they had fossilized.

The researchers could see it had a beaky head that looked a lot like a parrot—tall in height but short in length. One big difference, though, was that it had cheekbones that looked like horns sticking out from each side of its face.

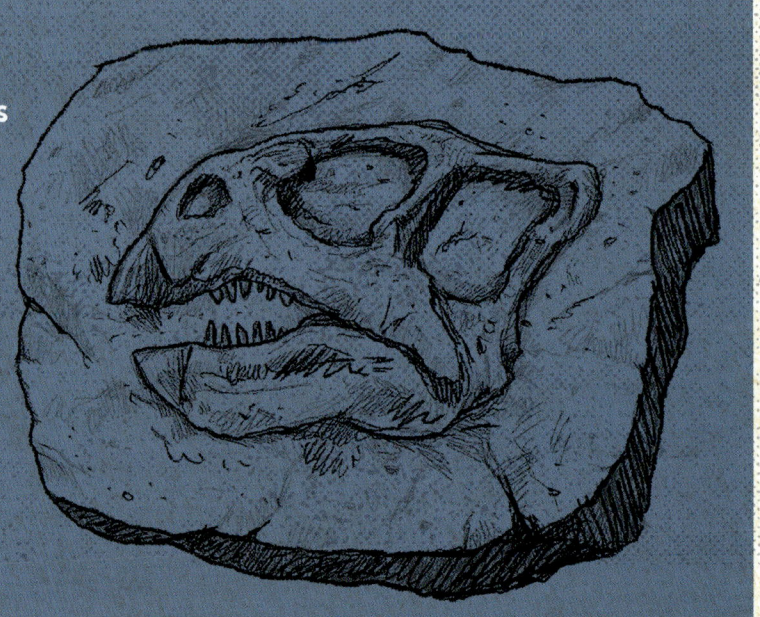

Dinosaur Belly Buttons

Psittacosaurus had a belly button! While it was growing in the egg, the dinosaur got its nutrients from a yolk sac. Before hatching, the yolk sac separated, leaving behind a scar (similar to our belly buttons). This makes *Psittacosaurus* the first known dinosaur with a belly button (also known as an umbilicus).

Psittacosaurus umbilicus

WHAT WE KNOW NOW

Today, *Psittacosaurus* is one of the best known dinosaurs. Hundreds of skeletons have been found.

Paleontologists now know that *Psittacosaurus* had very thick skin, and it swallowed small round stones ("gastroliths") to help grind up its food. Like modern birds, some dinosaurs had extra muscles in a part of their stomach to smash up food with the gastroliths—like a built-in garbage disposal!

In 2016, a team of scientists used lasers to figure out the colors of *Psittacosaurus*'s skin. They found it was light on the bottom and dark on the top. This coloring, also known as countershading, helped the animal blend in with its surroundings and hide from predators.

(veh-LOSS-ih-RAP-tore)
"SWIFT THIEF"

VELOCIRAPTOR

What do you imagine when you hear the name *Velociraptor*? Does the dino stand face-to-face with human adults, or barely reach their knees? Does it have feathered wings or hands that can open a kitchen door? The *Jurassic Park* and *Jurassic World* versions of *Velociraptor* are iconic, but the movie dinos were much larger and more reptile-like than the real animal.

Fast Facts

WHEN IT LIVED: Late Cretaceous (about 75 to 71 million years ago)		**WHERE FOSSILS FIRST FOUND:** Mongolia
LENGTH: About 6 feet (1.8 m)	**WHAT IT ATE:** Meat	
WEIGHT: About 33 pounds (15 kg)	**NAMED BY:** Henry Fairfield Osborn in 1924	

FIRST IMPRESSIONS

The very first *Velociraptor* skull was found next to a skull of a *Protoceratops*—almost 50 years before another pair would be found fossilized in combat (see "The Fighting Dinosaurs" on page 56).

The *Velociraptor* skull measured just seven inches (about 18 cm) long, but its mouth was full of pointy teeth. This first *Velociraptor* find also had its characteristic large curved claw, but paleontologists thought the claw was on its hand and used for pinning down prey. They also thought it was a close relative of *Megalosaurus* (like most carnivorous dinosaurs at the time).

Velociraptor had **LONG LEGS** and a **LONG, STIFF TAIL**, which helped it run fast.

WHAT WE KNOW NOW

We now have many good examples of *Velociraptor* skeletons. From those skeletons, researchers figured out that the famous claw was on its foot and not its hand.

Velociraptor probably did use its foot claws to pin down prey, and then tore into its prize with its many sharp teeth.

In 2007, scientists found quill knobs (bumps on the bone where large feathers attach) on the arm bone of a *Velociraptor*. Based on those bumps and newer discoveries of other feathered dinosaurs, paleontologists now think *Velociraptor* was covered with feathers. It also had wings and a tail fan, making *Velociraptor* more like a ferocious six-foot (1.8 m)-long turkey than a big scaly reptile.

Velociraptor kept its **KILLING CLAW** off the ground to keep it as sharp as possible.

DINO BATTLES

Life as a dinosaur was not easy. Lucky for us, some well-preserved fossils have given us a glimpse at their often violent struggles to survive.

THE FIGHTING DINOSAURS

One of the most famous preserved dino fights, found in Mongolia, is known as the "Fighting Dinosaurs" (creative name!): *Protoceratops* and *Velociraptor* individuals fossilized at the very moment of their battle to the death.

So who was winning? At first glance, the much heavier *Protoceratops* seems to have had the upper hand. The small dinosaur with a frill has *Velociraptor* pinned to the ground, with *Velociraptor*'s right hand in its jaws. However, *Velociraptor*'s hands are clutching *Protoceratops*'s skull, and *Velociraptor* has its feet— and sharp claws—pointed at *Protoceratops*'s belly and throat.

We'll never know who would have won—they may have even killed each other! Or they were killed together by a sand dune collapsing on them. Either way, the day ended badly for both of them.

Scientists may not know for sure how these two dinosaurs died, but they think they died together.

Over 70 million years ago, *Protoceratops* and *Velociraptor* were locked in a fight to the death. Moments later, they both perished and started the long process of fossilizing.

THE DUELING DINOSAURS

In Montana, fossil hunters found *Tyrannosaurus* and *Triceratops* individuals that died and were quickly buried together. Known as the "Dueling Dinosaurs," these two are like a supersize version of the Fighting Dinosaurs.

Both of them are still encased in rock (as of this writing, anyway), and so are their secrets, for now. But it's certainly possible they were in fact dueling!

Scientists already know a little bit about these two dinosaurs, including these details:

- The *Tyrannosaurus* fossil revealed the dino had a broken finger.
- There's a *Tyrannosaurus* tooth in the *Triceratops*'s spine.
- The *Tyrannosaurus* dino is missing most of its teeth.

Does this mean they were sparring? No spoilers yet: We'll have to wait to find out.

The tyrannosaur from the Dueling Dinosaurs is tentatively identified as *T. rex,* but it could be another tyrannosaur. We'll see what comes out of the rock!

OVIRAPTOR

Poor *Oviraptor*. It's probably one of the most misunderstood dinosaurs. With a name that means "egg thief," it's easy to get the wrong impression. But *Oviraptor* may not have even eaten eggs, let alone stolen them! And certainly not the eggs it was found with.

Eggs-quisite Nesting Sites

Dinosaurs had different strategies for laying their eggs. Some, like *Oviraptor*, sat on their eggs to keep them warm (and some, like *Troodon*, could even change their body temperature as needed).

Others had to get creative. For example, sauropods were too big to sit on their eggs, so they buried them to keep them warm. One of the largest sauropod nest sites ever discovered in Argentina was found near a place where there were ancient hot springs. There is evidence that the sauropods came back to nest every year, to keep their eggs in moist, warm soil.

Oviraptor cares for its young

Fast Facts

WHEN IT LIVED:
Late Cretaceous (about 75 to 71 million years ago)

LENGTH:
About 5 feet (1.5 m)

WEIGHT:
About 73 to 88 pounds (33 to 40 kg)

WHAT IT ATE:
Still being debated; possibly a mix of plants and meat

NAMED BY:
Henry Fairfield Osborn in 1924

WHERE FOSSILS FIRST FOUND:
Mongolia

FIRST IMPRESSIONS

Oviraptor was small and had a birdlike, toothless beak and large claws on its hands.

The man who named *Oviraptor*, Henry Osborn, knew the name might give the poor dino a bad reputation. In his description, he even wrote that the "egg thief" name might be misleading, especially when it came to what *Oviraptor* ate. However, he chose it because the first *Oviraptor* skeleton was found lying on top of a nest of dinosaur eggs. Specifically, Osborn thought the nest belonged to the horned dinosaur *Protoceratops*.

It all looked suspicious, very much like the dinosaur had died in a sandstorm while it was in the middle of stealing some eggs.

WHAT WE KNOW NOW

Oviraptor **found redemption in the 1990s.** Several discoveries showed that instead of stealing eggs, *Oviraptor* was probably taking care of its own eggs.

How did paleontologists figure this out? Researchers found a few *Citipati* skeletons (a close relative of *Oviraptor* that lived around the same time and place) lying on top of nests. They also found an embryo inside one of the eggs, which helped the researchers identify these nests as probably belonging to *Citipati*.

Both *Citipati* and *Oviraptor* were probably brooding, or keeping their eggs warm until they hatched. They were being good parents, not thieves!

The sharp points in OVIRAPTOR'S mouth aren't teeth. They're actually part of the palate!

THERIZINOSAURUS

There once was a dinosaur nearly as big as *T. rex,* but instead of short arms, it had the largest claws of any animal ever to walk on Earth.

That's how *Therizinosaurus* got the name "scythe lizard." But even though it had huge, menacing claws, we've learned that *Therizinosaurus* was more of a danger to plants than to other animals.

That's because *Therizinosaurus* was actually a herbivore, and its claws were way too long to use for fighting. They may not have been good for anything other than showing off to other therizinosaurs, intimidating predators, or possibly grabbing branches full of leaves.

Fast Facts

WHEN IT LIVED: Late Cretaceous (about 70 million years ago)		**WHERE FOSSILS FIRST FOUND:**
LENGTH: About 30 feet (9 m)	**WHAT IT ATE:** Plants	Mongolia
WEIGHT: About 5 tons (5 t)	**NAMED BY:** Evgeny A. Maleev in 1954	

FIRST IMPRESSIONS

Originally scientists thought *Therizinosaurus* was an epic sea turtle—one of the largest to swim on Earth. Evgeny A. Maleev, the paleontologist who named it, estimated *Therizinosaurus* to be 11 feet (3.5 m) long and 7 feet (2 m) wide. The original description even includes a drawing of a creature that resembles a sea turtle, with huge, webbed claws that could work as both flippers and scoops for eating seaweed.

The first *Therizinosaurus* find was basically just a few bone fragments, and one enormous claw measuring about two feet (60 cm) long. These bones were mixed with those of other animals, which is why Maleev thought he had found a giant sea turtle.

We still don't have many *Therizinosaurus* **bones,** but in 2009, scientists found a nearly complete skeleton of its close relative *Nothronychus*.

Nothronychus had short, stumpy legs with small feet—not good for swimming or chasing down prey. All it could manage was slowly walking from plant to plant. In addition,

it had wide hips, to make room for its large gut. The same would have been true for *Therizinosaurus*.

Both dinosaurs had a digestive system that worked basically like a big compost heap, and they needed time to break down all the plants they ate (which could be a smelly process).

Therizinosaurus would have been huge and very intimidating—but probably only dangerous if you got in between the dinosaur and the plants it wanted to gobble up.

THERIZINOSAURS ate plants, but most of their closest cousins (including T. rex) ate meat.

MAMENCHISAURUS

Do you take the bus to school? If *Mamenchisaurus* stuck its head through the back of your bus, it would easily be able to bite the steering wheel at the front.

That's because about half of this dinosaur's body was its neck. Luckily, its bones were mostly empty inside, so the neck was light enough that the dinosaur could hold its head up.

Fast Facts

WHEN IT LIVED: Late Jurassic to Early Cretaceous (about 161 to 114 million years ago)

LENGTH: Up to about 85 feet (26 m)

NAMED BY: C. C. Young in 1954

WEIGHT: Up to about 66 to 88 tons (60 to 80 t)

WHAT IT ATE: Plants

WHERE FOSSILS FIRST FOUND: China

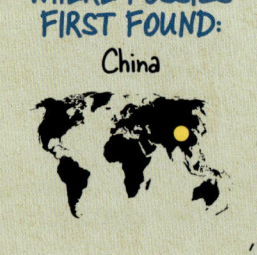

FIRST IMPRESSIONS

When paleontologists first named *Mamenchisaurus*, they didn't know just how long its neck was.

Different species of *Mamenchisaurus* had different neck lengths. Scientists estimated the first *Mamenchisaurus* named had a neck that was about 15 feet (4.5 m) long. The next *Mamenchisaurus* they named had a neck that was about 31 feet (9.3 m) long. For a while, with each new discovery, the neck seemed to grow!

Mamenchisaurus was the opposite of its relative *Diplodocus*. While *Mamenchisaurus* had an extreme neck, *Diplodocus* had an extreme tail. They lived in different parts of the world, so there must have been advantages for long necks in some places and long tails in others.

Mamenchisaurus had **THE LONGEST** known **NECK** of any dinosaur, with one measuring 49.5 feet (15.1 m) long!

In 2013, scientists re-created a *Mamenchisaurus* neck to test just how the dinosaur could actually hold it up. They found out the neck was not very flexible. They also learned that *Mamenchisaurus* most likely kept its neck horizontal and straight. However, the dinosaur could lower its head and neck to eat plants close to the ground.

Why would it need such a long neck? *Mamenchisaurus* wouldn't have had to move its heavy body around as much to get to its food, saving the dino a lot of time and energy.

MAJUNGASAURUS

You'd better hide if *Majungasaurus* is in the vicinity! It probably didn't run very fast (so maybe you could try to outrun it), but it had a strong skull built for killing prey.

Majungasaurus had a wide, rounded snout, with a powerful bite. It probably had a couple of tricks up its sleeve when it came to ambushing large sauropods, like *Rapetosaurus*. Just a few large bites could be enough to do major damage, and it could hold on tight even if a big dinosaur was flopping around. Moral of the story: Size won't save you from *Majungasaurus*!

Majungasaurus on the prowl

Fast Facts

WHEN IT LIVED: Late Cretaceous (about 70 to 66 million years ago)		
LENGTH: About 20 to 23 feet (6 to 7 m)	NAMED BY: René Lavocat in 1955	WHERE FOSSILS FIRST FOUND: Madagascar
WEIGHT: Roughly 0.8 ton (0.7 t)	WHAT IT ATE: Meat 	

FIRST IMPRESSIONS

The first *Majungasaurus* fossils were discovered in 1896. Only a few bones were found, including two teeth, a tail bone, and a claw. Paleontologists thought they were from *Megalosaurus*.

It took a long time to learn what the dinosaur's skull looked like. In 1979, scientists finally found a chunk of the top of the skull. That piece was dome-shaped, though, so at the time they thought it belonged to a pachycephalosaur.

Dino Eat Dino

Today, so many *Majungasaurus* bones have been dug up that we pretty much know what the whole skeleton looked like. Some of those skeletons were found in bone beds, full of *Majungasaurus* individuals.

Scientists learned a lot from these skeletons, including that *Majungasaurus* was a cannibal!

Some of the bones had very noticeable tooth marks on them, which matched up with *Majungasaurus* teeth. So yes, *Majungasaurus* ate other *Majungasaurus*. What's not clear, however, is whether they actually hunted each other, or just scavenged.

Majungasaurus isn't the only cannibalistic dinosaur: *Allosaurus* and *Tyrannosaurus* also show signs of eating their own kind—as many animals do today.

WHAT WE KNOW NOW

In the 1950s, someone found part of a jawbone while they were out collecting yams. Paleontologists compared it to the teeth found in 1896 and learned that what they first thought were *Megalosaurus* fossils were actually a new dinosaur: *Majungasaurus*.

Even more *Majungasaurus* fossils were found in 1996, including a nearly complete skull. Scientists saw that it had a somewhat dome-shaped head, just like the piece of skull that was found in 1979. So *Pachycephalosaurus* wasn't the only one with a thick head!

Now we know *Majungasaurus* had a small, round horn on the top of its head and short arms but sturdy legs.

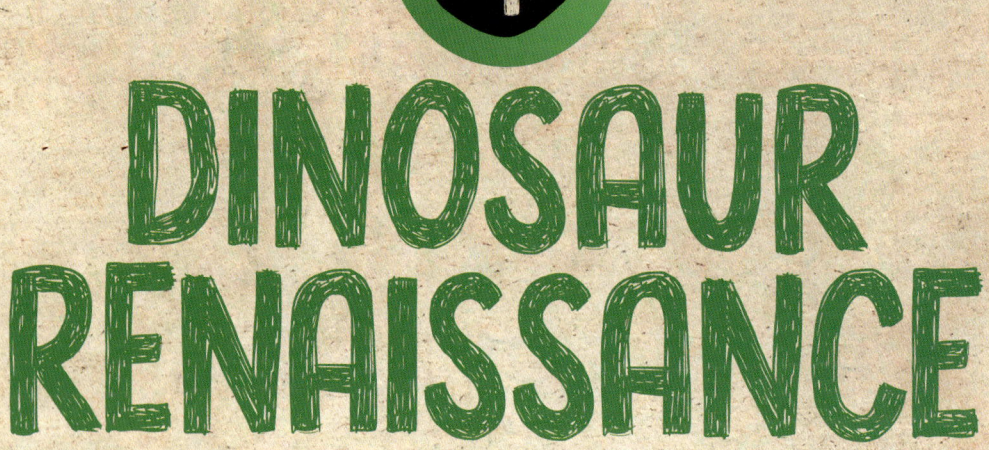

DINOSAUR RENAISSANCE

<mark>Large, lumbering lizards. For a long time, that's what most people thought dinosaurs were like.</mark>

Then in the 1960s, that all changed.

Paleontologist John Ostrom discovered *Deinonychus:* a fast-running, active predator (and relative of *Velociraptor*). Turns out dinosaurs weren't slow-moving and dumb. They were birdlike, warm-blooded, and active.

This period of time changed how we think about dinosaurs and inspired lots of scientists to study them in new ways. It also saved the word "dinosaur." Many scientists had stopped using that word because of an idea that dinosaur species weren't closely related. Fortunately, in 1974, paleontologists Robert Bakker and Peter Galton recognized key similarities between the different dinosaur groups, and brought back the word "dinosaur." What they didn't know was that in Argentina, José Bonaparte, known as the father of Argentinian paleontology, was coming to the same conclusions.

People started getting excited about dinosaurs again, which led to the discovery of more dinosaurs, which led to more excitement and even more discoveries! New museums dedicated to prehistoric life also started popping up, like the Royal Tyrrell Museum in Canada, which paleontologist Philip Currie helped found.

The Dinosaur Renaissance was mostly about rethinking dinosaurs that were described in earlier periods. However, two of the most misunderstood animals in the entire dinosaur family tree were discovered during this time: *Deinocheirus* and *Dilophosaurus*.

Left:
Watch out, John Ostrom!

Below left:
During this time, the term "paleoart" emerged, which combines art and science to illustrate prehistoric life. In this image, modern paleo–artist Júlia d'Oliveira displays her work.

Below right:
José Bonaparte, a pioneer of Argentinian paleontology and the man who named *Carnotaurus*, excavates an egg in Patagonia, Argentina.

DEINOCHEIRUS

One of the weirdest-looking dinosaurs, *Deinocheirus* had extremely large arms that ended with big claws on its hands for digging up plants. It also had a ducklike bill like a hadrosaur, a weak jaw, and no teeth. Can you picture Jar Jar Binks from *Star Wars*? That's pretty close to *Deinocheirus*.

Fast Facts

WHEN IT LIVED: Late Cretaceous (about 70 million years ago)

LENGTH: About 36 feet (11 m)

WEIGHT: About 8 tons (7 t)

WHERE FOSSILS FIRST FOUND: Mongolia

NAMED BY: Halszka Osmólska and Ewa Roniewicz in 1970

WHAT IT ATE: Plants and fish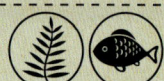

If You Think *Deinocheirus* Sounds Strange ...

Dinosaurs have always inspired creativity. The less we know about a dinosaur, the more inventive people get.

In 1899, author Frank Savile wrote the science fiction novel *Beyond the Great South Wall: The Secret of the Antarctic*. In the book he describes Cay, a meat-eating *Brontosaurus* sauropod, with

- a huge, lizard-like body;
- a neck like a boa constrictor;
- a heavy tail that dragged behind it, leaving a snail-like smear;
- four great flippers; and
- tusklike teeth.

Can you imagine? Today, we know sauropods were plant-eating dinosaurs that lived on land and had column-like legs and small teeth.

FIRST IMPRESSIONS

Paleontologist Zofia Kielan-Jaworowska found the first *Deinocheirus* fossils in 1965. She is famous for her explorations of the Gobi, a desert in Mongolia, where she discovered many mammals and dinosaurs, including the Fighting Dinosaurs (see page 56).

But she only found a pair of *Deinocheirus*'s gigantic arms (almost eight feet [2.4 m] long!) and a few other bones, such as parts of the ribs. It took decades to find anything more.

For almost 50 years, this dinosaur was a big mystery. Scientists described it as "bizarre" and "enigmatic." Many researchers thought *Deinocheirus* was similar to *Allosaurus*, but with souped-up arms that could tear apart prey with its large hands. Some scientists thought *Deinocheirus* was like a giant sloth and that it used its arms to climb trees.

When *Deinocheirus* was first described, paleontologists thought it was an ornithomimosaur, a group of dinosaurs known for being ostrichlike.

turn the page for more on *Deinocheirus*

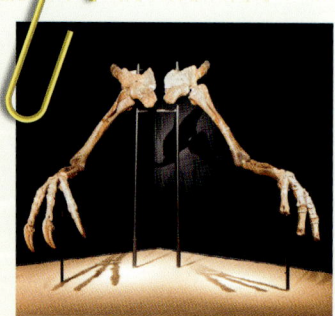

Enormous *Deinocheirus* arms

Coming Back Home

In 2008, a group of scientists found the site where *Deinocheirus* was first discovered. They dug up new bones, including two new skeletons. Now there were enough bones to know what the full skeleton of *Deinocheirus* looked like!

But one of the skeletons was missing the skull, hands, and feet. Poachers had taken them and smuggled the fossils out of Mongolia.

Luckily for the team, someone notified a paleontologist, who recognized the missing *Deinocheirus* skull in a private collection in Europe. Its skull, hands, and feet turned out to match the first new skeleton. In 2014, the fossils were "repatriated," or returned to Mongolia, where they could be properly studied.

Fossil poaching is taking fossils illegally from a dig site. Science is hurt by poaching. Not only do scientists miss out on studying the bones, but we also lose a lot of information about the dinosaur, like where and when exactly the dinosaur lived, even if the bones are recovered later.

Deinocheirus was bulky, but having **HOLLOW BONES** helped keep it light.

WHAT WE KNOW NOW

When the new skeletons were finally discovered, *Deinocheirus* went from mysterious and terrifying to goofy almost overnight. Instead of powerful jaws full of sharp teeth, it had a hadrosaur-like bill and probably ate mostly soft plants. Its large, scary arms wouldn't have helped it slash and kill prey. They were more like giant salad tongs it used to scoop up food.

Paleontologists confirmed that *Deinocheirus* was an ornithomimosaur, but it had a lot of strange features, partly because it was so big. For example, it had

- a hump or a sail on its back;
- a fan of feathers on its tail;
- a large skull, with a deep jaw, to hold its big tongue;
- enormous, hooved feet that may have kept it from sinking when wading in mud;
- short legs; and
- wide hips, to help support its weight and create space for lots of plant-digesting intestines.

Additionally, scientists found more than a thousand gastroliths with *Deinocheirus*, which were stones it probably swallowed to help grind up food in its gut. They found fish bones and scales, too, so *Deinocheirus* likely ate both plants and fish.

DILOPHOSAURUS

Would you be afraid of a dog-size, venom-spitting *Dilophosaurus* with a neck like a frilled lizard? Fortunately for you, it never existed! There isn't any evidence that *Dilophosaurus* could spit venom or had a neck frill, like it did in *Jurassic Park*.

Scientists briefly thought a dinosaur named *Sinornithosaurus* had a venomous bite because of its long, grooved teeth. However, they never thought it *spit* venom. And after closer inspection,

Sinornithosaurus teeth weren't all that special. So, like *Dilophosaurus*, it probably didn't have any venom at all.

But some birds, which are descended from dinosaurs, vomit their food as a way to drive away predators: Turkey vultures throw up food to defend themselves, and can fling their vomit up to 10 feet (3 m) away! (Although we get why *Jurassic Park* chose spitting acid over projectile vomiting.)

Fast Facts

WHEN IT LIVED: Early Jurassic (about 184 million years ago)		**WHERE FOSSILS FIRST FOUND:**
LENGTH: About 23 feet (7 m)	**WHAT IT ATE:**  Meat	Navajo Nation, Arizona, U.S.A.
WEIGHT: Up to 0.6 ton (0.5 t)	**NAMED BY:** Samuel P. Welles in 1970	

FIRST IMPRESSIONS

The first *Dilophosaurus* skeleton was found by a Navajo man named Jesse Williams in 1940, but paleontologists didn't name the dinosaur until 1954. At first, it was called *Megalosaurus wetherilli*.

Scientists thought *Dilophosaurus* was similar to *Megalosaurus*, but with longer arms and a longer lower leg. They only had an incomplete skull to work with, and it wasn't in the best shape, so they

didn't notice the animal's now famous pair of crests on top of its head.

The scientists measured its leg at more than four feet five inches (136 cm) long—large for a predator at the beginning of the Jurassic.

Dilophosaurus looks wrong without its head crests.

WHAT WE KNOW NOW

In 1964, paleontologists found a second, larger skeleton, which showed that the original *Dilophosaurus* was still growing when it died. By 1970, the dinosaur was famous for its unique head crests, which ran from its snout to its eyes. *Megalosaurus wetherilli* became *Dilophosaurus*

wetherilli to describe the dino's two impressive crests.

Today, *Dilophosaurus* is considered the largest and most ferocious animal that roamed North America in the Early Jurassic. Scientists reexamined its head crests, and they now think those crests grew even higher above its head. The two crests were probably filled with air, similar to those of hornbills, a modern tropical bird. *Dilophosaurus* may have used its crests to impress potential mates.

DILOPHOSAURUS'S cousin, *Monolophosaurus*, was also named for its crest, but it had just one.

5

DINOSAUR BLOCKBUSTERS

"Hold on to your butts!"

In 1993, the movie *Jurassic Park* inspired an entire generation of paleontologists. It showed dinosaurs as smart and fast—the way scientists had thought about them since the Dinosaur Renaissance.

As a result, dinosaurs became so cool that more people started searching for them and studying them around the world. Professional and amateur fossil hunters alike began looking much more closely at dirt around their homes. Most didn't find any fossils, but some found marvelous specimens of their favorite dinosaurs, while others found brand-new species. Researchers even searched for DNA in dinosaur fossils. Unfortunately, attempts to re-create a dinosaur from DNA failed—and it's unlikely we're going to be able to resurrect dinosaurs anytime soon.

As of 1994, dinosaurs had officially been found on all seven continents: Paleontologists named the carnivorous theropod *Cryolophosaurus,* a dinosaur from Antarctica known for the fancy pompadour-style crest on top of its head. (Life found a way.)

Computers helped make the dinosaurs on screen even more exciting. In 1999, *Walking With Dinosaurs* used digital animation to show dinosaurs interacting in real environments around the world. But computers did more than help make great dinosaur movies. Scientists started scanning the inside of bones, figuring out bite forces, and even learning dinosaurs' colors— a whole new world of scientific possibility was opening up.

T. rex could bite with a force of at least 35,000 newtons (about four tons). Enough to shatter bones!

Digital scan of a *Triceratops* skull

Digitally modeling a dinosaur foot

(MAH-no-NIGH-kus)
"ONE CLAW"

MONONYKUS

If you've ever seen a roadrunner, you have a good idea of what *Mononykus* (and other members of its family, the alvarezsaurids) looked like. This two-legged dinosaur had a long tail—though much longer than a roadrunner's—and was quick on its feet.

One big difference? Instead of wings, *Mononykus* had tiny arms with a huge claw on each hand.

Fast Facts

WHEN IT LIVED: Late Cretaceous (about 70 million years ago)

LENGTH:	NAMED BY:	WHERE FOSSILS FIRST FOUND:
About 3 feet (1 m) long	Perle Altangerel and three other researchers in 1993	Mongolia
WEIGHT: Almost 9 pounds (4 kg)	**WHAT IT ATE:** Insects	

FIRST IMPRESSIONS

The first alvarezsaurid finds were incomplete and hard to identify. For example, when two alvarezsaurid leg bones were first discovered, researchers thought the bones belonged to large owls. *Mononykus* was named about 20 years later, and it had a much more complete skeleton. The find included an amazing set of mysterious arms. The arms were clearly powerful but short and ended abruptly in large claws. The claws were so big they were even larger than their arms!

At first, scientists thought *Mononykus* could burrow, but they've since figured out its arms were too short, and its body was built more for running than digging.

Scientists also thought *Mononykus* was a bird. It was fluffy and very birdlike—down to the shape of its leg, neck, and back bones. Even its hip bone pointed backward, like a bird's.

WHAT WE KNOW NOW

We've learned that although alvarezsaurids looked a lot like birds, they evolved their birdlike features completely on their own. They are actually closer relatives of *Therizinosaurus* than of birds.

As more alvarezsaurids were discovered, it became clear these dinosaurs all belonged in a group together. One of the new dinosaurs discovered, *Shuvuuia*, had three fingers, but two of its fingers were so small they were pretty much useless. Like its relatives, *Shuvuuia* could only use one finger.

Why did *Mononykus* and its relatives have such large claws but short arms? We've learned that early alvarezsaurids probably couldn't dig very well, but they could grasp prey. Later alvarezsaurids evolved to have more specialized arms and claws, and could probably break holes through hard mud, termite mounds, or anthills with their claws, and then scoop up the insects in their jaws. Paleontologists don't know, however, if they had a long, sticky tongue like an anteater!

What's funny is that alvarezsaurids might have a connection to owls after all. A recent study of an alvarezsaurid skull found that its eyes and ears were similar to owls'. Maybe, like owls, it had good hearing and hunted at night.

CLAWS: NATURE'S HANDY TOOLS

A lot of mammals, reptiles, and birds today have nails or claws. And just like these animals, dinosaurs also had a wide variety of claws.

Claws come in different lengths and can be curved or straight, sharp or blunt. How animals use their claws depends on these kinds of features. They can, however, be used for multiple purposes (like grabbing food and lounging in trees).

Scientists mainly use two methods to figure out how dinosaurs used their claws. They compare their claws to modern animals with similar claws or they test dinosaur claws in different situations to see how well they perform at different tasks.

A few clues they look for include:

- Claws with more of a curve are better for climbing.
- Flatter claws are better for running and jumping.
- The thicker the base of the claw, the stronger the grip force.
- Long, thin, and curved claws make it easier to pierce into prey.

Check out these charts for some of the ways modern animals and dinosaurs used their claws.

ANIMAL	THEY USE THEIR CLAWS TO ...
Aardvarks	Dig in the dirt
Kangaroos	Launch themselves while hopping
Lions	Cling to prey like Velcro
Ostriches	Defend against predators
Parasitic jaegers	Steal food from other birds
Ravens	Perch on trees
Sloths	Hang from branches
Woodpeckers	Climb trees

Sloth

The sickle-shaped claws on *Velociraptor's* second toes stay off the ground, to help keep them sharp.

Velociraptor on the prowl for prey

DINOSAUR	THEY USED THEIR CLAWS TO ...
Haplocanthosaurus (a sauropod)	Dig nests (back foot claws)
Linhenykus (an alvarezsaurid)	Shovel for insects
Megaraptor (a megaraptorid)	Skewer large prey
Therizinosaurus (a therizinosaurid)	Attract mates or grab leaves
Velociraptor (a dromaeosaurid)	Pin prey

Sloth claw

One thing to keep in mind: Claws can change as animals grow into adults. For example, baby three-toed sloths use their claws to cling to their mothers. As they grow up, their claws get longer, and the sloths use them as hooks to hang from tree branches.

Some baby birds (also known as living dinosaurs) have small claws on the front edge of their wings that they lose as they get older. These claws help them climb steep branches to escape predators that invade their nests.

(YOU-taw-RAP-tore)
"UTAH THIEF"

UTAHRAPTOR

Nineteen ninety-three was a great year for dinosaur fans. *Jurassic Park* became the biggest movie of all time! It showed fast, powerful, and intelligent raptors chasing down helpless humans. At the same time, paleontologists were in the desert near Arches National Park in Utah, digging up *Utahraptor* bones that closely resembled the raptors on the big screen.

Fast Facts

WHEN IT LIVED: Early Cretaceous (about 130 to 124 million years ago)	**WHERE FOSSILS FIRST FOUND:** Utah, U.S.A.

LENGTH: About 20 feet (6 m)	**WEIGHT:** About half a ton (0.4 t)	**WHAT IT ATE:** Meat 

NAMED BY: James Kirkland, Donald Burge, and Robert Gaston in 1993

FIRST IMPRESSIONS

Picture Blue, the scaly *Velociraptor* from *Jurassic World*. That's pretty much what scientists originally thought *Utahraptor* looked like. James Kirkland, who named *Utahraptor*, even joked that *Utahraptor* is the real animal in the first *Jurassic Park* movie, although the real *Utahraptor* was even more ferocious—its killing claw was longer and straighter, which made it a better weapon.

Utahraptor was the largest dromaeosaurid (the group informally called "raptors") by far when it was found. Its killer toe claw bone was about 9.4 inches (24 cm) long! That's twice as long as the raptor with the previous record, *Deinonychus*. *Utahraptor* also had narrow hand claws, perfect for cutting. When it was first discovered, scientists also thought it had scaly skin.

Just three years after *Utahraptor* was named, paleontologists described the first non-avian dinosaur with feathers (*Sinosauropteryx*). Shortly after that, researchers found *Microraptor* completely covered in fossilized feathers. Because many relatives of *Utahraptor* have been found with feathers, scientists' best guess is that *Utahraptor* was also covered in feathers, not scales.

A Utahraptor Trap

The *Utahraptor* Megablock is a nine-ton (8-t) block of sandstone that's full of hundreds of *Utahraptor* bones from over a dozen individuals! It's possible they fell into a predator trap. In this case, they probably were trying to eat a herbivorous dinosaur stuck in quicksand (dinosaurs never passed up a seemingly easy meal!). *Utahraptor* after *Utahraptor* was drawn to the quicksand, where they were buried and fossilized. In 2021, the site where all the dinosaurs were found became part of the new Utahraptor State Park in Grand County, Utah, U.S.A.

Fossils from the megablock

GIGANOTOSAURUS

Who would win in a fight, *T. rex* or *Giganotosaurus*? They were both huge predators with massive heads full of sharp teeth, and they both had comically small arms.

The answer is definitely *T. rex*, but it's a trick question. *Giganotosaurus* was already long gone or fossilized by the time *T. rex* walked the Earth! The last *Giganotosaurus* individual died almost 30 million years before *Tyrannosaurus* evolved. You could pretty easily win a fight against a dinosaur skeleton, too.

Meraxes gigas

Fast Facts

WHEN IT LIVED: Late Jurassic (about 154 to 152 million years ago)

LENGTH: About 43 feet (13 m)

WEIGHT: About 8 tons (7 t)

WHAT IT ATE: Meat

NAMED BY: Rodolfo A. Coria and Leonardo Salgado in 1995

WHERE FOSSILS FIRST FOUND: Argentina

FIRST IMPRESSIONS

Giganotosaurus was a formidable animal. At the time it was discovered, it was the largest predatory dinosaur ever found in the Southern Hemisphere.

The skull alone was more than five feet (1.5 m) long. That estimate was based on a good set of jaws and part of a skull, but the space between them took a little guesswork. Scientists had an easier time estimating *Giganotosaurus*'s body length since they'd found a lot of the spine.

Real-World Dragons

Fossils may have inspired legendary creatures like dragons and griffins. It's easy to see why: Dinosaurs often had terrifying teeth, chilling claws, and were stupendous in size.

Scientists like science fiction and fantasy stories, too. Sometimes names from those stories make their way into dinosaur names. For example,

- *Meraxes*, the *Giganotosaurus* relative named after a dragon from *Game of Thrones*;
- *Thanos*, the *Carnotaurus* relative named after the Marvel character;
- *Dracorex hogwartsia*, the "dragon king of Hogwarts Academy" (which may actually be a juvenile *Pachycephalosaurus*); and
- *Gojirasaurus*, the Triassic predator named after Godzilla.

WHAT WE KNOW NOW

In 2022, scientists described *Meraxes gigas,* a close relative of *Giganotosaurus* and the most complete skeleton of a carcharodontosaurid (a group of large carnivorous dinos) ever found in the Southern Hemisphere. *Meraxes* helped fill in a lot of gaps in our knowledge about *Giganotosaurus.*

For example, based on the *Meraxes* skull, scientists figured they had underestimated the size of the *Giganotosaurus* skull (by about four inches [10 cm]). Now they think the skull was five feet four inches (163 cm) long. *Meraxes* also had very small arms. So, like *T. rex, Giganotosaurus* had a very large head but unimpressive arms—although *Giganotosaurus* probably had three fingers.

SINOSAUROPTERYX

Even long after the discovery of the feathered (and birdlike) dinosaur *Archaeopteryx*, scientists thought of dinosaurs as more crocodile-like than bird-like. *Sinosauropteryx* changed all that. When paleontologists discovered *Sinosauropteryx*, they presented it to John Ostrom (from the Dinosaur Renaissance). He teared up when he saw it because the find confirmed his life's work, proving that some non-avian dinosaurs (dinosaurs that aren't birds) had feathers.

Fast Facts

WHEN IT LIVED: Early Cretaceous (about 124 to 122 million years ago)

LENGTH: Up to about 3.5 feet (1 m)

WEIGHT: About 2 pounds (1 kg)

WHAT IT ATE: Meat

WHERE FOSSILS FIRST FOUND: China

NAMED BY: Qiang Ji and Shu'an Ji in 1996

FIRST IMPRESSIONS

Sinosauropteryx had a very long tail made up of 64 BONES!

At first, scientists thought that *Sinosauropteryx* was a bird (which would still technically make it a dinosaur because all birds evolved from dinosaurs). *Sinosauropteryx* had features that were similar to both birds and non-avian theropods—the group of mostly predatory dinosaurs known for having three toes and claws on their hands and feet.

Some paleontologists also thought that *Sinosauropteryx* had a frill of skin along its neck, back, and tail. They suggested the structures that made the frill were collagen fibers (tissue found in skin).

After studying the fossils more closely, paleontologists noticed the details in the halo around *Sinosauropteryx* looked much more like feathers than a frill made of skin (and the feathers were short and small).

Sinosauropteryx also has the honor of being the first dinosaur whose color we know! It had a cool look with several stylish features, including

- a reddish and white banded tail;
- a raccoon-style bandit mask on its face; and
- a body that was darker on the top and lighter on the bottom ("countershading").

With these markings, *Sinosauropteryx* was well suited to camouflage itself in open spaces. This would have helped it hide from both predators and prey. (Also helpful was that it could run very fast on its two legs, like an ostrich.)

How Do We Know Dinosaur Colors?

Melanosomes are structures in a cell that determine both the color of dinosaur feathers and our hair. Melanosomes tend to have different shapes for each color. Scientists can therefore look at fossilized mela-nosomes under a microscope, and based on the shape, can sometimes tell the fossil's color. They do this by comparing melanosomes in living animals to fossils.

MEGARAPTOR

The most mega things about *Megaraptor* are its claws. The first claw found was three times as long as a grizzly bear's claw, and that didn't even include the tip. Paleontologists estimated the full claw bone was more than 14 inches (37 cm) long, and that still wasn't even the entire claw—it was only the bony part (which is true of every dinosaur claw you see at a museum).

Fast Facts

WHEN IT LIVED: Late Cretaceous (91 to 88 million years ago)

WHERE FOSSILS FIRST FOUND: Argentina

LENGTH: About 26 feet (8 m)

WEIGHT: About 2 tons (2 t)

WHAT IT ATE: Meat

NAMED BY: Fernando E. Novas in 1998

FIRST IMPRESSIONS

Scientists originally found only four *Megaraptor* bones: an arm bone, a long finger bone, a partial foot bone, and its fantastic claw, which would've been even larger in life than as a fossil. Animals' claw bones are covered with keratin, which makes them bigger than the bones alone. Keratin doesn't usually fossilize, so researchers don't know exactly how long a *Megaraptor* claw was, but it probably would have been over 16 inches (40 cm), a little bigger than a bowling pin!

The sharp cutting edge on the bottom of the claw and the grooves on the sides looked like the foot claws of raptors like *Velociraptor*, so scientists thought the *Megaraptor* claw also came from its foot.

The other bones are larger than the matching bones in *Allosaurus*. Paleontologists thought *Megaraptor* was larger than *Allosaurus*, with very large hands and a huge killing claw on its foot.

Does this claw look out of place?

WHAT WE KNOW NOW

Despite its name, *Megaraptor* was not a raptor, and it's a pretty distant relative of *Velociraptor.*

Just four years after *Megaraptor* was named, paleontologists dug up a more complete skeleton (including, most important, a complete hand!). The first finger ended in a claw that looked nearly identical to the claw scientists thought was a foot claw (talk about keeping them on their toes).

They realized that *Megaraptor* had its impressive claw on its hand and not its foot (and raptors are known for their foot claws), which made the name pretty misleading. This mix-up is the opposite of what happened with *Velociraptor* (originally researchers thought the *Velociraptor* toe claw was a hand claw). Figuring out whether a dinosaur's claw is from a foot or hand is really difficult without more bones.

(MY-crow-RAP-tore)
"SMALL THIEF"

MICRORAPTOR

If you could fly, would you rather have two wings or four? *Microraptor* had so many feathers on its arms and legs that scientists think it had four wings! (And if you include the stiff feathered tail, maybe even five wings). Having so many wings might actually have made it harder for *Microraptor* to fly, though.

Microraptor is small, but it is nowhere near the smallest dinosaur. Because birds are dinosaurs, the smallest dinosaur ever to live is the bee hummingbird. They're so small, their eggs are the size of a coffee bean!

Fast Facts

WHEN IT LIVED: Early Cretaceous (about 125 to 120 million years ago)		WHERE FOSSILS FIRST FOUND: China
LENGTH: About 2 to 3 feet (0.6 to 1 m)	**WEIGHT:** Up to about 4 pounds (2 kg)	**WHAT IT ATE:** Meat
NAMED BY: Xu Xing, Zhonghe Zhou, and Xiaolin Wang in 2000		

FIRST IMPRESSIONS

The first *Microraptor* found was, as it turned out, mixed in with two other types of dinosaurs (making the combination a "chimera" or "composite").

At first, people thought this composite was a missing link between dinosaurs and birds. But paleontologists quickly figured out that only the tail belonged to *Microraptor,* and the other bones belonged to a prehistoric bird, *Yanornis,* and an unnamed animal.

Researchers keep debating whether or how well *Microraptor* could fly. At first, they thought *Microraptor* would have stuck to gliding between trees, because the wings on its legs were attached to its feet, which would have made running difficult.

Citipati osmolskae

A Broody Bunch

Though no *Microraptor* nests have been found (yet), some scientists think this dinosaur may have used its four wings to keep its eggs warm—also known as brooding. The idea isn't too far-fetched, especially when dinosaurs like *Citipati* have been found sitting on top of their nests. If it's true, *Microraptor* probably sat in the middle of the nest, letting its feathery arms and legs cover its eggs.

The debate on how well *Microraptor* could fly continues. Luckily for us, fossil hunters have found more than 300 *Microraptor* skeletons, so we now know a lot of other details about this dinosaur! We know the following about *Microraptor*:

- The dinosaur had feet like a hawk's, with spiky scales and strong foot joints to help it grip prey (potentially small dinosaurs and small pterosaurs).

- It also ate mammals, fish, and lizards, which scientists found fossilized in their guts! It's unclear whether the dinosaur hunted or scavenged its food.
- It was covered in black, iridescent feathers, based on its melanosomes (see page 85), looking similar to birds alive today. It would have looked beautiful in the sunlight.
- It could probably climb trees and had long legs that may have helped it run fast.
- It molted like a songbird, shedding a few feathers at a time (which may mean it flew around a lot, looking for food or escaping from predators).

DINOSAUR ANIMATION

Dinosaurs have been an important part of animated films since before movies had sound. In 1914, Gertie was born: a cheerful sauropod (probably *Brontosaurus*) and the first animated dinosaur—acting like an enormous trained elephant. She playfully wagged her tail, rolled over, and performed other tricks.

Other animated dinosaurs rampaged through cities *(The Lost World)*, fought cowboys *(The Valley of Gwangi)*, or went on adventures with each other *(The Land Before Time)*.

Every dinosaur depiction got more people thinking about paleontology, and the biggest films *(King Kong* and *Jurassic Park)* made even more people excited about studying dinosaurs. What these new scientists learned then influenced what dinosaurs looked like in later movies. Early animations mostly show dinosaurs as slow, lumbering, and not very smart. But after the Dinosaur Renaissance (see page 66), the dinosaurs became much faster and more intelligent, and they had better posture.

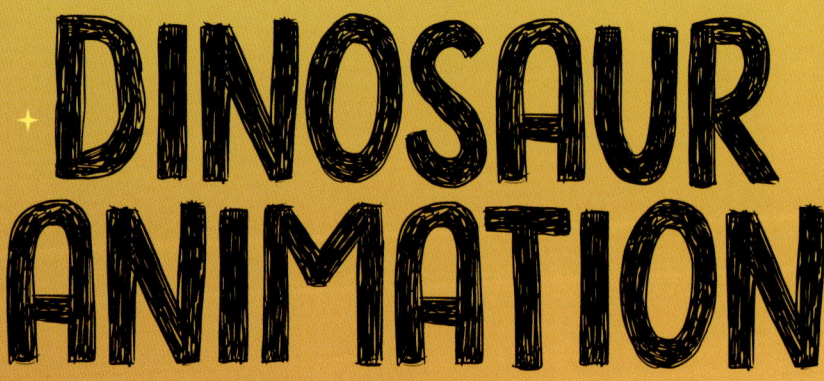

King Kong (left 1933; right 2005): Features an epic battle between a three-fingered tyrannosaur and King Kong.

Jurassic Park (1993): Using the most scientifically accurate dinosaur animations of its time, the film features Rexy, a fast-running and smart tyrannosaur.

Gertie the Dinosaur (1914): Stars a cartoon sauropod so large she can drink an entire lake and swallow a tree whole.

The Dinosaur and the Missing Link: A Prehistoric Tragedy (1915): A sauropod with a low snakelike neck and tail makes an appearance.

The Ghost of Slumber Mountain (1918): Features dinos (Triceratops) with hippo-shaped bodies fighting each other until a Tyrannosaurus individual spoils the party.

Along the Moonbeam Trail (1920): Shows Stegosaurus flicking a forked, snakelike tongue while hunting people on the moon.

The Lost World (1925): A tail-dragging killer dino (Brontosaurus) destroys London.

Fantasia (1940): Shows Brachiosaurus diving into a lake to escape Tyrannosaurus (at the time, scientists thought sauropods spent most of their time in water).

The Animal World (1956): Features a carnivorous Brontosaurus individual that was mostly aquatic.

The Valley of Gwangi (1969): Wild West cowboys wrangle a tail-dragging Allosaurus with a powerful tail and legs.

When Dinosaurs Ruled the Earth (1970): Shows a baby sauropod, as cute as it is inaccurate, with a very large head and feet.

Prehistoric Beast/Dinosaur! (1985): Building on work from the Dinosaur Renaissance, it's the first animation to include Tyrannosaurus in its modern posture—back parallel to the ground and tail not dragging.

Walking With Dinosaurs (1999): Nature documentary-style series that set a new bar in scientific accuracy of dinosaur animation. Shows a herd of Iguanodon individuals walking on four legs and running on two.

Jurassic Park III (2001): Features a dinosaur that was supposedly Spinosaurus, but it was a little bit too tall and powerful.

Jurassic World (2015): Emphasized potential pack hunting of raptors (aka "raptor training").

Prehistoric Planet (2022): Features Tyrannosaurus with lips.

The Land Before Time (1988): The dinosaur Spike (Stegosaurus) spends most of his time eating, like a real stegosaur.

6

THE GOLDEN AGE

Open your window. Did you hear that? It's the sound of a new dinosaur being discovered. Well, maybe not really. But there is a good chance someone out there is currently digging up a new dinosaur.

We live in the golden age of dinosaur discovery. A new species of dinosaur is named almost every week! Now we know of over a thousand species of dinosaurs, with probably hundreds more left to discover.

For many years, most paleontologists came from just a few countries and they would travel around the world to find new fossils. Today, scientists all over the world are starting programs in their home countries. For example, paleontologist Xu Xing has made a huge impact on the study of feathered dinosaurs in China. And there are ongoing efforts in Brazil, Egypt, Mongolia, and many other fossil-filled countries that are sure to foster more paleontologists (and ultimately lead to new dinosaur discoveries).

After all these new finds, some of the dinosaur species named in the past turned out not to be "valid." That means scientists either figured out a dinosaur was actually the same as a dinosaur already named, or there weren't enough fossils found of a particular dinosaur to know for sure.

Keep reading to learn about some recently discovered dinosaurs, and how their fossils helped fill in gaps in our knowledge.

Above right: Dr. Lindsay Zanno in her lab

Above left: Dr. Aubrey Jane Roberts fossil hunting

Below left: Dr. Bolortsetseg (Bolor) Minjin with a juvenile *Tarbosaurus* skull

Researchers dig up fossils in Utah, U.S.A.

YUTYRANNUS

Yutyrannus was a fluffy dinosaur, covered in feathers. Sounds cute, right? Don't let the fluff fool you! It was a gigantic predator, similar in size to large tyrannosaurs that lived millions of years later.

Though this meat-eating theropod was only distantly related to *Tyrannosaurus*, it still had a large, powerful skull, a mouth full of teeth, and sharp claws.

Fast Facts

WHEN IT LIVED: Early Cretaceous (about 125 million years ago)		
LENGTH: About 25 feet (7.5 m)	**WEIGHT:** About 1.4 tons (1.3 t)	**WHERE FOSSILS FIRST FOUND:** China
NAMED BY: Xu Xing and eight other researchers in 2012	**WHAT IT ATE:** Meat 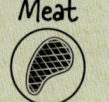	

FIRST IMPRESSIONS

Before *Yutyrannus* was discovered, paleontologists didn't think large carnivorous dinosaurs had any feathers. *Yutyrannus* changed that idea overnight. It weighed 40 times more than the previous largest dinosaur with feathers, *Beipiaosaurus*.

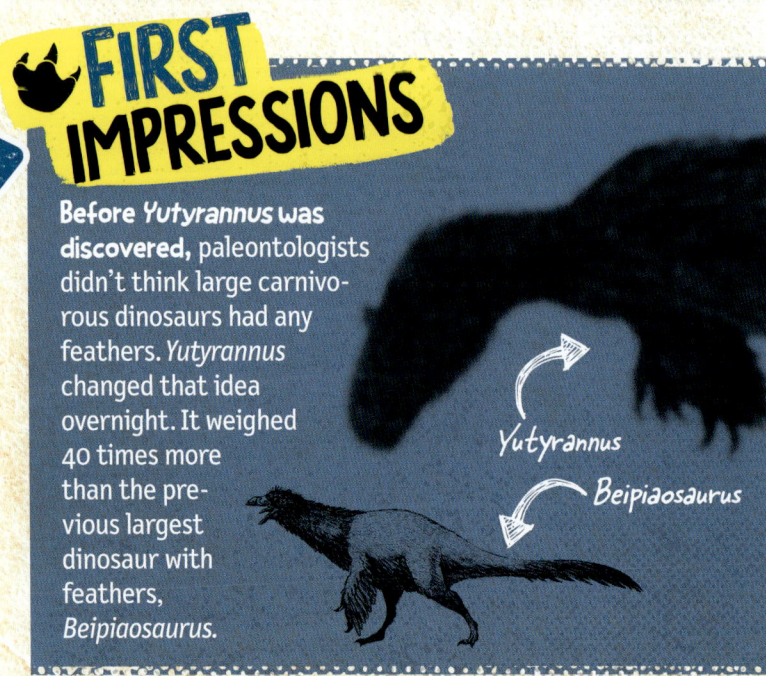

Yutyrannus

Beipiaosaurus

Fluffing feathers

Practical Plumage

Feathers can be useful for both warming up and cooling down. We see this with birds today: Birds that live in colder environments have more fluffy feathers to keep in heat. Longer feathers can create a thicker layer to trap warm air near the body.

But birds can also use their feathers to cool down during hot summer days. They can puff up and fluff out their feathers to get rid of hot air pockets, or hold up their wings and use them like a parasol. Dinosaurs with feathers would have done the same thing. They lived all over the world, so some would have appreciated the added insulation while others would have liked the built-in shade.

WHAT WE KNOW NOW

Scientists discovered three *Yutyrannus* **skeletons.** Between these specimens, they found feathers on the tail, feet, hips, arms, and neck. This means it is likely that *Yutyrannus* was completely covered in feathers.

The types of feathers found on *Yutyrannus* were very long, with some measuring almost eight inches (20 cm). These feathers may have helped keep *Yutyrannus* warm—useful in its relatively cold climate, where temperatures averaged 50°F (10°C).

Because *Yutyrannus* was so large and had so many feathers, paleontologists now think that its relatives may have also been feathered. Possibly even *T. rex*, though this thought has ruffled a few feathers!

BOREALOPELTA

In 2011, a large machine at a mine hit something very hard. The operator saw bits of bone and skin preserved in the rock. They were from an ankylosaur, the most heavily armored of all the dinosaurs.

The *Borealopelta* individual had fossilized in a concretion (hard rock), which helped protect it. In a way, *Borealopelta* had even stronger armor as a fossil than it did when it was alive.

Fast Facts

WHEN IT LIVED: Early Cretaceous (about 110 to 112 million years ago)			**WHERE FOSSILS FIRST FOUND:** Alberta, Canada

LENGTH: About 18 feet (5.5 m)	**NAMED BY:** Caleb Brown and seven other researchers in 2017	**WHAT IT ATE:** Plants	
WEIGHT: About 1.4 tons (1.3 t)			

FIRST IMPRESSIONS

From first sight it was clear that *Borealopelta* **was much more important than a typical dinosaur discovery.** Once the rock was removed, it looked like a stone sculpture of a dinosaur, complete with skin, armor, and even facial features exactly as they were when the dinosaur was buried.

Before *Borealopelta*, paleontologists weren't sure what might have covered the armored bumps and spikes, also known as osteoderms, on ankylosaurs. *Borealopelta*, with its 172 preserved osteoderms, changed all that! All of them are covered in keratin, which is rarely fossilized.

This keratin extends well beyond the end of the spines, making the spines much larger than the bones themselves suggest. And up until this discovery, scientists had only studied the bones.

Scientists now realized other ankylosaurs probably had even longer and bigger spikes and armor than they had thought.

WHAT WE KNOW NOW

Paleontologists have learned a lot from the *Borealopelta* discovery, including what color it was. Based on studying chemicals in the fossils, scientists found that *Borealopelta* was reddish-brown on its back and lighter on the bottom. This coloring, called countershading, allowed it to camouflage. Although *Borealopelta* was covered in threatening spikes and armor, it still needed to hide from predators.

The excavator that discovered *Borealopelta* broke off a chunk of the fossil. At first, it seemed like the damage was a disappointing side effect of the discovery. But there was a silver lining: Paleontologists could see its fossilized guts (a "cololite")! They were able to confirm *Borealopelta* swallowed a lot of rocks (gastroliths) to grind up food in its stomach, and in addition to eating plants, the dinosaur ate some charcoal and wood. It's possible *Borealopelta* was eating ferns in a forest that had recently burned.

HALSZKARAPTOR

Picture a swan, with its long, elegant neck. Now make its snout longer and full of closely packed teeth. Shorten its wings and add clawed fingers. Change the webbed feet into raptor-like feet, with extra-sharp, curved claws on each of its second toes. Last, make the tail much longer than a swan's tail feathers. That's *Halszkaraptor*—the scariest swan you've ever seen.

Fast Facts

WHEN IT LIVED: Late Cretaceous (about 75 million years ago)

LENGTH: About 3 feet (0.9 m)

WEIGHT: About 1.4 pounds (0.6 kg)

NAMED BY: Andrea Cau and nine other researchers in 2017

WHAT IT ATE: Possibly fish

WHERE FOSSILS FIRST FOUND: Mongolia

FIRST IMPRESSIONS

The paleontologists who named *Halszkaraptor* suggested this dinosaur spent a lot of time in the water hunting for fish. However, some key bones in the ribs that would prove it was a good swimmer were missing. So, scientists kept debating whether *Halszkaraptor* really was a good swimmer.

Others argued that *Halszkaraptor* had features just like other dinosaurs that spent all their time on land, including its long neck and sharp claws, and that there was not enough evidence *Halszkaraptor* looked for food underwater.

Some pointed out that *Halszkaraptor* had features like a crocodile, such as similar blood vessels and nerves in its snout and teeth that curved backward.

Halszkaraptor was a perplexing dinosaur, with characteristics that showed it could spend time on land and in the water.

WHAT WE KNOW NOW

In 2022, paleontologists named a new dinosaur and close relative to *Halszkaraptor: Natovenator.*

The name *Natovenator* means "swimming hunter," and its discovery helps fill in pieces missing from the *Halszkaraptor* skeleton. *Natovenator* had a barrel-shaped rib cage, which meant its body was adapted to easily move through water.

Like *Halszkaraptor, Natovenator* had a swanlike neck, which would have been useful for grabbing fish. Both dinosaurs also had short arms that may have worked like flippers.

Additionally, *Natovenator* had huge eyes, which would have helped it see underwater, where there's less light.

Because *Halszkaraptor* and *Natovenator* are closely related, and *Natovenator* probably was a good swimmer, it seems likely that *Halszkaraptor* was a good swimmer as well.

Though *HALSZKARAPTOR* looked like a scary swan, it was closer in size to a mallard duck!

BAJADASAURUS

The award for the dinosaur with the best mohawk goes to ... *Bajadasaurus!* This small sauropod had long spines that ran down its neck and back and curved forward into a C-shape. Like the spines of *Spinosaurus,* this dinosaur's spines are actually the top part of the backbone.

It's hard to imagine how *Bajadasaurus* would have moved its neck around without those extremely tall neck bones causing problems. It must have had a very good reason to have such radical spines!

Fast Facts

WHEN IT LIVED: Cretaceous (about 140 to 133 million years ago)

LENGTH: About 30 to 40 feet (9 to 13 m)

WEIGHT: About 2 to 4 tons (2 to 4 t)

NAMED BY: Pablo A. Gallina and three other researchers in 2019

WHAT IT ATE: Plants

WHERE FOSSILS FIRST FOUND: Argentina

FIRST IMPRESSIONS

Bajadasaurus **is a dicraeosaurid,** a sauropod group known for having relatively small bodies, short necks, and long spines on their necks and backs.

At first, scientists thought the spines poked through the dinosaur's skin, and the parts that stuck out were covered in keratin that formed horns. The spines had ring-shaped ridges on them, similar to an antelope. So they thought *Bajadasaurus* would have had pairs of large antelope-like horns down its neck and back.

Bajadasaurus with menacing black horns

In 2022, a team of researchers studied the spines of *Amargasaurus,* a close relative of *Bajadasaurus* that's also famous for the large spines on its neck. The spines were bifurcated, meaning they were split into two. This was very unusual for an animal with such long spines. Other animals with long spines, like *Spinosaurus,* only had single spines.

The scientists wanted to know: What did those spines really look like? Were they horns, or something else, like a pair of *Spinosaurus* sails or a camel hump?

They took pieces from *Amargasaurus*'s neck and back and compared them to animals that have horns, crests, and humps.

They learned the ring-shaped ridges on the spines were from where the spines had broken. That meant the spines probably weren't horns. The researchers also found evidence of skin attached to the spines.

But a hump would have been too heavy for *Amargasaurus* and its relatives. That means *Bajadasaurus* probably had a pair of sails on its neck. We still don't know exactly why it had neck sails. They could have been for attracting mates, intimidating rivals, deterring predators, or all of the above.

STEGOUROS

Stegouros was about the size of a basset hound, but it was much stranger than any dog breed. Like other ankylosaurs, it had a beak for chomping tough plants and bony armor for protecting its body.

However, *Stegouros* had a very bizarre tail—even for an ankylosaur. Its broad, powerful tail was covered in seven pairs of large triangular spikes, all fused together.

Fast Facts

WHEN IT LIVED: Late Cretaceous (about 72 to 75 million years ago)

LENGTH:
About 5 to 5.5 feet (1.5 to 1.7 m)

WEIGHT:
About 180 pounds (80 kg)

WHAT IT ATE:
Plants

NAMED BY:
Sergio Soto-Acuña and 20 other researchers in 2021

WHERE FOSSILS FIRST FOUND:
Última Esperanza, Chile

FIRST IMPRESSIONS

Before *Stegouros*, ankylosaurs were split into two groups:
- ankylosaurids, with impressive tail clubs like *Ankylosaurus*, and
- nodosaurids, with no club, but usually impressive shoulder spikes, like *Borealopelta*.

Stegouros revealed there were ankylosaurs that didn't fit into either group. Paleontologists named a new group, Parankylosauria, which includes dinosaurs from Chile, Antarctica, and Australia.

In the Early Cretaceous, the continents were still connected in a supercontinent called Gondwana. It's possible that all the parankylosaurians, including *Antarctopelta* in Antarctica and *Kunbarrasaurus* in Australia, had impressive *macuahuitl*-style tails (see box at right).

The Macuahuitl

Stegouros had a formidable tail weapon that was similar to the *macuahuitl*, a wooden club the size of a flattened baseball bat, with blades embedded in the sides. The blades were made of sharpened obsidian—black volcanic glass that was also used for arrowheads. Macuahuitls were fierce weapons. In Meso-america, civilizations like the Aztec and Maya often used them because they could cut flesh and fracture bone. Macuahuitls could also leave behind flakes of obsidian that would make it harder for wounds to heal and possibly lead to infection.

Warriors with macuahuitls

WHAT WE KNOW NOW

Over 70 million years before Meso-americans were using macuahuitls in battle, *Stegouros* had evolved a similar weapon built into its tail. The only *Stegouros* individual paleontologists have found so far was about as long as a green sea turtle, even as an adult. Compared with a turtle, the dinosaur would have weighed much less, stood on slender legs, and had a tail that ended in a solid foot (30 cm) of jagged weaponry.

UNSOLVED MYSTERIES

We may never know everything there is to know about dinosaurs. In fact, we definitely won't. Here are some mysteries scientists are still working on solving.

Ambopteryx

THE "STRANGE WING" DINOSAUR

Paleontologists have only found one *Yi* skeleton. This dinosaur lived in the Late Jurassic, about 159 million years ago, in what is now China. *Yi* was small, weighing less than 14 ounces (380 g).

What makes *Yi* so mysterious is a massive rodlike bone sticking out of its wrist. Paleontologists' best guess is that it was covered in skin like the wing of a bat or pterosaur.

Just a few years after *Yi* was found, another dinosaur with a similar extra wrist bone was discovered—*Ambopteryx*. Even with two dinosaurs, it's still unclear how that wrist bone was positioned and how capable of flying they were.

In 2020, a team of researchers found that the wings of *Yi* and *Ambopteryx* were unique compared to other winged dinosaurs that lived around the same time as them.

The researchers came to the conclusion that these dinosaurs couldn't fly like birds today. But their wings still would have been useful for gliding between trees in a forest canopy. We need more discoveries to better understand this unusual group of animals.

Yi

Concavenator

THE "HUMPBACKED HUNTER" DINOSAUR

Paleontologists knew from the beginning that *Concavenator* **was bizarre.** *Concavenator* lived in the Early Cretaceous, about 130 million years ago, in what is now Spain. It was a medium-size carnivorous theropod, at almost 20 feet (6 m) long. This dino had bumps on its short arms—scientists are still debating whether it had short, stiff, feather-like bristles on its arms or whether the bumps were related to muscle scars.

What makes it stand out, though, are its two long neural spines—tall bones that poked up from the top of the backbones, or vertebrae. Most dinosaurs with these long spines had more of them—several situated in a row, forming a hump or sail over most or all of their back (like *Spinosaurus*).

But not *Concavenator*. Because there were only two spines, it had only a small bump above its hips.

Why? Perhaps the spines formed a hump that helped store energy, or maybe it was a sail that helped keep the dino cool, or made it look cool to attract potential mates.

Hopefully in the future, researchers will find more *Concavenator* fossils, and we can unlock the secrets of its seriously strange back.

What's Next for Dinosaurs

The golden age of dinosaur discoveries continues because more people around the world are becoming interested in dinosaurs. New museums, movies, books, and games have really helped! So has access to dinosaur science. It makes a difference to have fossil hunters in countries where people hadn't previously been looking.

There are many great science communicators around the world, eager to share their love of dinosaurs. Whether that's through movable museums, like the Institute for the Study of Mongolian Dinosaurs run by paleontologist Bolor Minjin, online videos and games like those created by scientists Aline Ghilardi and Tito Aureliano, or podcasts (wink, wink), there's something for everyone.

Let's keep solving those mysteries.

DINO MAP

Dinosaurs thrived on all seven of today's continents, and as a result, their bones can be found all over the planet! Dinosaurs are listed in the location where they were first discovered. This map only shows the dinosaurs mentioned in the book, but dinosaur bones (or at least teeth) can be found almost everywhere on Earth.

NORTH AMERICA

PACIFIC OCEAN

SOUTH AMERICA

SOUTHERN OCEAN

Europe

Cetiosaurus (England)
Hylaeosaurus (England)
Iguanodon (England)
Megalosaurus (England)

Archaeopteryx (Germany)

Concavenator (Spain)

North America

Canada:

Anodontosaurus (Alberta)
Borealopelta (Alberta)
Brachylophosaurus (Alberta)
Centrosaurus (Alberta)
Corythosaurus (Alberta)
Daspletosaurus (Alberta)
Edmontosaurus (Alberta)
Lambeosaurus (Alberta)
Parasaurolophus (Alberta)
Regaliceratops (Alberta)
Saurolophus (Alberta)
Styracosaurus (Alberta)

Mexico:

Tlatolophus (Coahuila)
Velafrons (Coahuila)

United States:

Dilophosaurus (Arizona)

Allosaurus (Colorado)
Apatosaurus (Colorado)
Brachiosaurus (Colorado)
Camarasaurus (Colorado)
Ceratosaurus (Colorado)
Diplodocus (Colorado)
Haplocanthosaurus (Colorado)
Stegosaurus (Colorado)
Triceratops (Colorado)
Torvosaurus (Colorado)

Hesperornis (Kansas)

Podokesaurus (Massachusetts)

Ankylosaurus (Montana)
Deinonychus (Montana)
Einiosaurus (Montana)
Maiasaura (Montana)
Pachycephalosaurus (Montana)
Troodon (Montana)
Zuul (Montana)

Hadrosaurus (New Jersey)

Coelophysis (New Mexico)
Nothronychus (New Mexico)
Gojirasaurus (New Mexico)

Diabloceratops (Utah)
Kosmoceratops (Utah)
Utahraptor (Utah)

Brontosaurus (Wyoming)
Camptosaurus (Wyoming)
Dryosaurus (Wyoming)
Tyrannosaurus (Wyoming)

South America

Alvarezsaurus (Argentina)
Amargasaurus (Argentina)
Bajadasaurus (Argentina)
Giganotosaurus (Argentina)
Megaraptor (Argentina)
Meraxes (Argentina)

Thanos (Brazil)

Stegouros (Chile)

ARCTIC OCEAN

EUROPE

ASIA

AFRICA

PACIFIC OCEAN

Asia

China:

Ambopteryx
Beipiaosaurus
Linhenykus
Mamenchisaurus
Microraptor
Shunosaurus
Sinornithosaurus
Sinosauropteryx
Tsintaosaurus
Yutyrannus
Yi

Mongolia:

Citipati
Deinocheirus
Halszkaraptor
Mononykus
Natovenator
Oviraptor
Protoceratops
Psittacosaurus
Shuvuuia
Therizinosaurus
Velociraptor

Russia:

Amurosaurus
Olorotitan

Africa

Spinosaurus (Egypt)

Majungasaurus (Madagascar)
Rapetosaurus (Madagascar)

Spicomellus (Morocco)

Giraffatitan (Tanzania)

OCEANIA

AUSTRALIA

Antarctica

Antarctopelta
Cryolophosaurus

Australia

Kunbarrasaurus

ANTARCTICA

GLOSSARY

Bonebed: a layer of rock full of bones, usually from multiple animals

Brooding: the process of keeping eggs warm until they hatch

Centrosaurines: a group of ceratopsian dinosaurs generally known for their large nose horns, short frills, and short horns above their eyes

Ceratopsians: a group of plant-eating dinosaurs with beaks

Chasmosaurines: a group of ceratopsian dinosaurs generally known for their short nose horns, long frills without spikes, and long horns above their eyes

Chimera or composite: describing a dinosaur skeleton composed of a mix of bones from different dinosaurs

Collagen fibers: strong microscopic threadlike structures that add strength to skin, bones, and other plant and animal tissues

Cololite: fossilized gut contents

Concretion: hard solid rock formed around something (like a fossil)

Coprolites: fossilized poop

Countershading: a pattern of coloring of an animal's body that is darker on the top and lighter on the bottom, to offset sunlight and help camouflage it from predators

Desiccation and deflation: the drying out of an animal, such as a dinosaur, without it fully decomposing, resulting in the skin collapsing onto the bones before the dinosaur is buried

Dinosaur mummy: a fossil that is well-preserved enough to include pieces of skin and other things that don't usually fossilize, such as keratin

Gastroliths: small round stones some dinosaurs swallowed to help grind up their food (animals like alligators, some birds, and even sea lions still do this today)

Hadrosaurs: a group of plant-eating dinosaurs known for their duck bill–like snouts

Keratin: the substance that makes up fingernails, hair, and feathers, and covers an animal's horns and claws

Lambeosaurines: a group of hadrosaurs known for their large hollow head crests

Melanosomes: specialized structures in a cell that determine the color of dinosaur feathers (and our hair, skin, and eyes)

Molting: the shedding by an animal of old feathers, hair, skin, or even a shell, to make room for new growth

Non-avian dinosaur: a dinosaur that isn't a bird or close relative to modern birds, including all of the dinosaurs in this book other than *Hesperornis* and (probably) *Archaeopteryx*

Olfactory bulb: a structure in the brain that helps with the sense of smell

Osteoderms: bones that grow directly in the skin separate from the skeleton, including plates, bumps, spikes, or other shapes (often found with ankylosaurs and stegosaurs)

Quill knobs: bumps on the bone where large feathers attach

Sauropods: a group of generally large four-legged dinosaurs known for their long necks, long tails, and relatively small heads

Semiaquatic: animals that live partly on land and partly in water

Thagomizer: the spikes at the end of a stegosaur's tail

Theropods: a group of mostly predatory dinosaurs known for having three toes and sharp claws on their hands and feet

REFERENCES

Brett-Surman, Michael K., Thomas R. Holtz, and James O. Farlow. *The Complete Dinosaur.* Indiana University Press, 2012.

Holtz, Thomas R., Jr. *Dinosaurs: The Most Complete, Up-to-Date Encyclopedia for Dinosaur Lovers of All Ages.* Random House, 2007.

Ottaviani, Jim. *Bone Sharps, Cowboys, and Thunder Lizards: Edward Drinker Cope, Othniel Charles Marsh, and the Gilded Age of Paleontology.* G.T. Labs, 2005.

Paul, Gregory S. *The Princeton Field Guide to Dinosaurs.* Princeton University Press, 2024.

Rhodes, Frank H.T., Paul R. Shaffer, Herbert S. Zim, and Raymond Perlman. *Fossils: A Fully Illustrated, Authoritative and Easy-to-Use Guide.* St. Martin's Press, 2001.

Ricci, Sabrina, and Garet Kruger. *I Know Dino: The Big Dinosaur Podcast.*

INDEX

PHOTO CREDITS

Illustrations by Franco Tempesta/© National Geographic Partners, LLC, unless otherwise noted below.

ASP: Alamy Stock Photo; NGIC: National Geographic Image Collection; SS: Shutterstock

COVER (tape), pics five/SS; (arrow), bioraven/SS; (paper background), ESB Professional/SS; (dino footprint), WinWin/Adobe Stock; (green circle), Sarunyu_foto/SS; **INTERIOR** Throughout: (paper clips), Blan-k/SS; (photo corners and frames), LiliGraphie/SS; (dino footprint), WinWin/Adobe Stock; (tape), pics five/SS; (paper background), ESB Professional/SS; (meat icon), Dmitr1ch/SS; (world map), Mike McNey, senior cartographer/NG Maps; (arrow), foxie/SS; (plant vector), Arc Tina/SS; (brush stroke circle), Sarunyu_foto/SS; (arrows), bioraven/SS; (dragonfly vector), Toseef Yousaf/SS; (fish vector), anthonycz/SS; 11 (UP LE), Science History Images/ASP; 11 (UP RT), SBS Eclectic Images/ASP; 11 (LO), Sueddeutsche Zeitung Photo/ASP; 13 (CTR RT), Historic Images/ASP; 14 (CTR), Oxford Science Archive/Print Collector/Getty Images; 18-19, Great Plains Dinosaur Museum & Field Station; 19 (UP), Daan Meens courtesy of North Dakota Geological Survey; 23 (UP LE), Heritage Image Partnership Ltd/ASP; 23 (UP RT), IanDagnall Computing/ASP; 23 (LO), Alpha Historica/ASP; 26 (CTR RT), Universal Images Group North America LLC/DeAgostini/ASP; 30 (LE), Stocktrek Images, Inc./ASP; 30 (RT Background), Herschel Hoffmeyer/SS; 31 (UP), Julius Csotonyi/Royal Tyrrell Museum; 33 (UP LE), From the Archives and Special Collections, Mount Holyoke College; 33 (UP RT), Paul Fearn/ASP; 33 (LO), Photo 12/ASP; 41 (RT), Tina Forbush; 43 (LO RT), Panther Media GmbH/ASP 45 (UP RT), Kat Keen Hogue/NGIC; 46 (UP RT), Nizar Ibrahim/NGIC; 50 (CTR LE), Universal Images Group North America LLC/DeAgostini/ASP; 50-51 (LO), Stocktrek Images, Inc./ASP; 51 (CTR RT), Sebastian Kaulitzki/Science Source; 51 (CTR RT background), Herschel Hoffmeyer/SS; 51 (LO RT), Michael Rosskothen/Adobe Stock; 53 (UP RT), Robert Clark/NGIC; 56 (UP), Francois Gohier/Science Source; 57 (UP RT), Mohamad Haghani/ASP; 57 (LO), Associated Press; 64, Daniel Eskridge/SS; 67 (UP), Louie Psihoyos; 67 (LO LE), Júlia d'Oliveira; 67 (LO RT), Louie Psihoyos; 70, Xavier Fores - Joana Roncero/ASP; 75 (UP), Robert Clark/NGIC; 75 (LO LE), Smithsonian Institute/Science Source; 75 (LO RT), Pascal Goetgheluck/Science Source; 78-79 (claw marks), Vector Tradition/SS; 78, Damsea/SS; 79 (LO), dam/Adobe Stock; 81 (CTR RT), Associated Press; 82, Science Photo Library/ASP; 88, Daniel Eskridge/Adobe Stock; 90-91 (filmstrip), Buch and Bee/SS; 90 (CTR LE), Archive PL/ASP; 90 (LO CTR), Maximum Film/ASP; 90 (LO RT), Photo 12/ASP; 91 (UP LE), Album/ASP; 91 (UP RT), Murray Close/Getty Images; 91 (CTR LE), United Archives GmbH/ASP; 91 (CTR CTR), Album/ASP; 91 (CTR RT), RGR Collection/ASP; 93 (UP LE), Victoria Engelschion Nash; 93 (UP RT), Joshua Steadman; 93 (CTR RT), Bolortsetseg Minjin; 93 (LO), Cory Richards/NGIC; 94, yonatan/Adobe Stock; 102, The Picture Art Collection/ASP; 105, Michael Rosskothen/ASP; 106-107, Mike McNey, senior cartographer/NG Maps

For our two amazing daughters, hatched while we wrote this book, and to dinosaur fans everywhere—may your curiosity never go extinct.

Since 1888, the National Geographic Society has funded more than 14,000 research, conservation, education, and storytelling projects around the world. National Geographic Partners distributes a portion of the funds it receives from your purchase to National Geographic Society to support programs including the conservation of animals and their habitats. To learn more, visit natgeo.com/info.

For more information, visit nationalgeographic.com, call 1-877-873-6846, or write to the following address:

National Geographic Partners, LLC
1145 17th Street NW
Washington, DC 20036-4688 U.S.A.

More for kids from National Geographic: natgeokids.com

National Geographic Kids magazine inspires children to explore their world with fun yet educational articles on animals, science, nature, and more. Using fresh storytelling and amazing photography, Nat Geo Kids shows kids ages 6 to 14 the fascinating truth about the world—and why they should care. natgeo.com/subscribe

For rights or permissions inquiries, please contact National Geographic Books Subsidiary Rights: bookrights@natgeo.com

Designed by Brett Challos

I Know Dino is a trademark of I KNOW DINO, LLC.

Hardcover ISBN: 978-1-4263-7553-8
Reinforced library binding ISBN: 978-1-4263-7564-4

The publisher would like to thank expert reviewers Aline Ghilardi and Tito Aureliano. Book team: Katharine Moore, senior editor; Sarah Gardner, photo editor; Katherine Kling, fact-checker; and David Marvin and Lauren Sciortino, associate designers.

Printed in South Korea
24/QPSK/1

Borealopelta

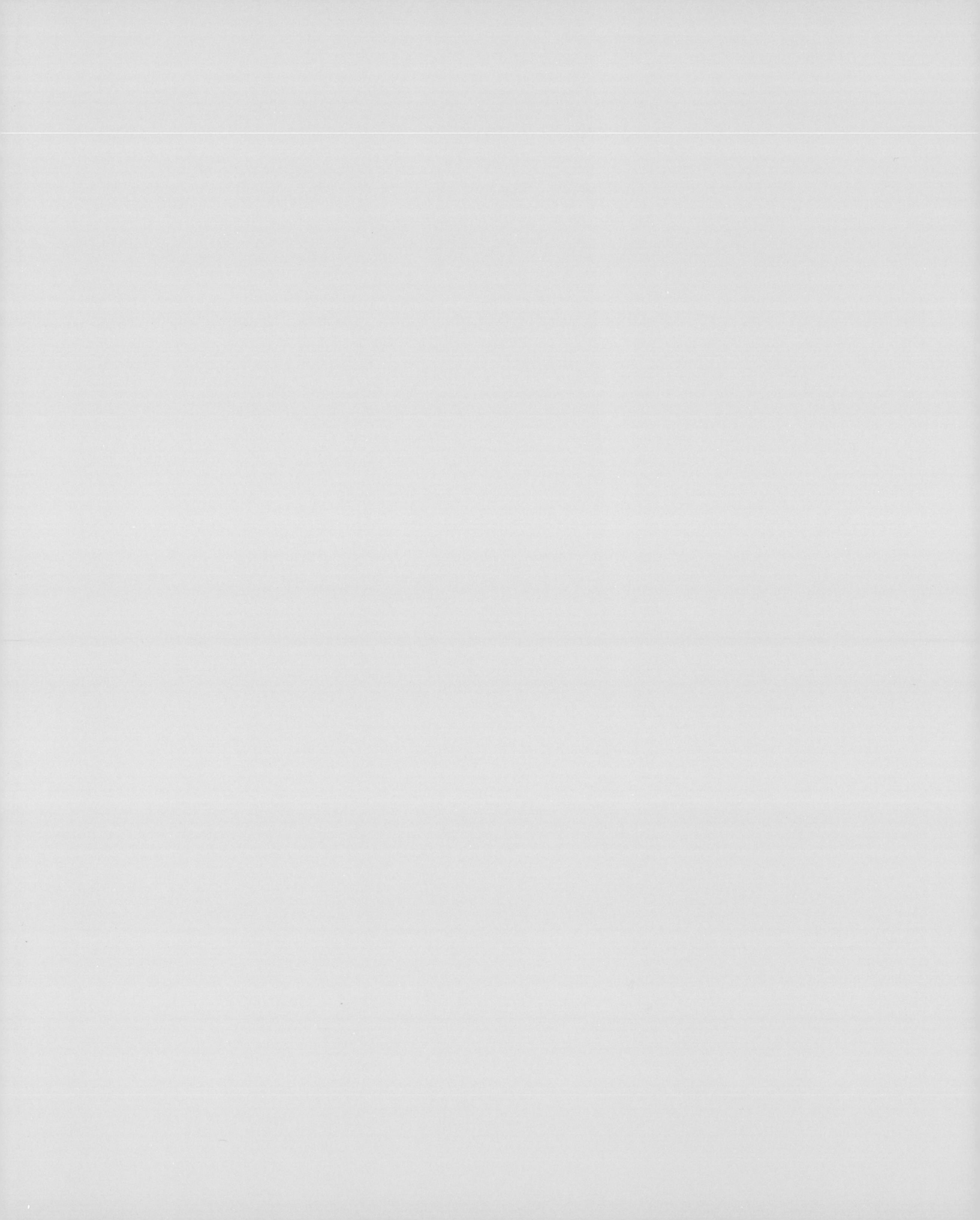